CAPTIVE RAPTOR

MANAGEMENT & REHABILITATION

Illustration: Elizabeth Darby

Captive Raptor

Management & rehabilitation

Richard Naisbitt & Peter Holz

hancock
house

ISBN 0-88839-490-X
Copyright © 2004 Richard Naisbitt, Peter Holz

Cataloging in Publication Data
Naisbitt, Richard, 1965–
    Captive raptor management & rehabilitation / Richard Naisbitt & Peter Holz.

Includes bibliographical references and index.
ISBN 0-88839-490-X

    1. Birds of prey. 2. Captive wild birds. 3. Birds of prey—Wounds and
injuries—Treatment. 4. Birds of prey—Diseases—Treatment.
I. Holz, Peter II. Title. III. Title: Captive raptor management and
rehabilitation.

QL677.78.N33 2004   639.9'789   C2004-904368-4

Editor: David Bender
Production: Bob Canlas, Ingrid Luters
Cover Design: Theodora Kobald
Illustrations: Richard Naisbitt, Elizabeth Darby
Photography: Richard Naisbitt, Matthew Kettle, Marcia Salverson

Published simultaneously in Canada and the United States by

HANCOCK HOUSE PUBLISHERS LTD.
19313 Zero Avenue, Surrey, B.C. V3S 9R9

HANCOCK HOUSE PUBLISHERS
1431 Harrison Avenue, Blaine, WA 98230-5005

(604) 538-1114   Fax (604) 538-2262
(800) 938-1114   Fax (800) 983-2262
Web Site: www.hancockhouse.com   *email:* sales@hancockhouse.com

CONTENTS

Appendix 2 Tables

List of Figures

INTRODUCTION

The subject of captive raptor management is not confined to the eagle in the aviary or the broken-winged kestrel, nor is it restricted to the falconer's bird on an ornate perch. Captive raptor management is about managing the bird in all conditions, from the rehabilitation front, to the demonstration field, to the hunting area. It is about keeping a raptor in captivity and maintaining its good health for the duration of its existence under these circumstances. This could mean a stay of only ten days in the case of birds undergoing rehabilitation for minor injury. But for those kept by the falconer, the display educator and zookeeper, it could mean up to twenty years, or even longer.

Raptor keepers, despite their individual objectives, should all share the ultimate goal of the correct application of management strategies that have been uniquely designed for each bird in their care. The demonstrator who employs a variety of raptors in a presentation aims to show the birds' skills by exploiting their natural range of behaviors. The zookeeper and aviculturist must keep their birds fit and healthy within the more limited habitat of an aviary. The rehabilitator needs to bring injured and/or unfit raptors back into good condition, or prepare orphans or starving individuals for release with a reasonable chance of survival. All these tasks are melded into *Captive Raptor Management*.

Vanessa and a peregrine

Illustration: Elizabeth Darby

CHAPTER ONE
RAPTOR SURVIVAL STRATEGIES

1.1 HUNTING TECHNIQUES

1.1.1 Overview

Basic hunting methods are hard-wired in virtually all raptors. The way in which each member of a given species forages for its prey does not vary from the Northern to the Southern Hemispheres. The prey selected might vary, but, with the exception of a few anomalies, the search and attack strategy is the same. The method by which a raptor hunts is governed by its physical attributes. The bird's wing-loading, tail length, tarsal length, and foot size all contribute to its choice of prey and its hunting methods.

Foraging or hunting in raptors involves both the search and attack strategies. However, for convenience, in many raptors the search itself seems to be more important, and the final act of "catching" the prey is almost passive. Here we think of the insect and rodent feeders, which we refer to as searchers. The extreme passive searchers are the vultures. Alternatively, then, are those species that usually exert great energy on the final chase and attack; these we shall refer to as attackers. They are the bird and larger mammal hunters (Fox 1995), exemplified by the peregrine falcon and the golden eagle.

Because of the fundamental behavioral differences and energy requirements between searchers and attackers, the rehabilitator, the demonstration exhibitor, or the falconer must approach these two groups with different rehabilitation, exercise, and training strategies. Searchers have a low wing-loading, making slow flight easy; they invariably employ a simple attack strategy and feed upon relatively abundant and slow-moving prey. The attackers are the reverse. They have a high wing-loading, often use complex attack strategies, and feed upon fast-moving prey that may or may not be abundant. There are always exceptions, and many raptor species employ a strategy that overlaps the two. Some raptors behave like searchers during their first year of life, then switch strategies, becoming attackers after their first molt. Having said the above, there are elements of searching and attacking employed by all raptors. For a more detailed account of raptor biology, see *Understanding the Bird of Prey* (Fox 1995).

Table 1.1.1 Comparable wing loadings.

Species	Scientific name	Wing loading	Searcher	Attacker	Diet	Distribution
Peregrine	*Falco peregrinus*	0.65	No	Yes	Birds	Cosmo
Black falcon	*F. subniger*	0.36	Yes	Yes	Birds/mammals	Aust
Brown falcon	*F. berigora*	0.33	Yes	No	Opportunistic	Aust
Lanner falcon	*F. biarmicus*	0.45	No	Yes	Birds/insects	Af/Eur
Saker falcon	*F. cherug*	0.53	Yes	Yes	Birds/mammals	Eur/AS
Gyrfalcon	*F. rusticolus*	0.78	No	Yes	Birds/mammals	NA/AS/Eur
European kestrel	*F. tinnunculus*	0.22	Yes	No	Insects/small rodents	Eur
American kestrel	*F. sparverius*	0.20	Yes	No	Insects/smallrodents	NA
Little falcon	*F. longipennis*	0.33	No	Yes	Birds	Aust
Merlin	*F. columbarius*	0.33	No	Yes	Birds	NA
Eur Red necked falcon	*F. chiquera*	0.36	No	Yes	Birds	Af/As
Prairie falcon	*F. mexicanus*	0.37	No	Yes	Birds/mammals	NA
Cooper's hawk	*Accipiter cooperii*	0.37	No	Yes	Birds/mammals	NA
Sharp-shinned hawk	*A. striatus*	0.24	No	Yes	Birds	NA
E. sparrow-hawk	*A. nisus*	0.32	No	Yes	Birds	Eur
Shikra	*A. badius*	0.22	Yes	Yes	Birds/small rodents/ insects	Af/As
Marsh harrier	*Circus aeruginosus*	0.30	Yes	No	opportunistic	Eur/Af/As/ Aust
Black-shouldered kite	*Elanus caeruleus*	0.25	Yes	No	Small rodents	NA/Af
Black kite	*Milvus migrans*	0.28	Yes	No	Opportunistic	Af/As/Eur/ Aust
Red -tailed hawk	*Buteo jamaicensis*	0.47	Yes	Yes	Opportunistic	NA
Rough-legged buzzard	*B. lagopus*	0.40	Yes	No	Mammals	NA/As/Eur
Common buzzard	*B. buteo*	0.45	Yes	No	Mammals	Eur/As
Red-shouldered hawk	*B. lineatus*	0.49	Yes	No	Birds/mammals	NA
Harris's hawk	*Parabuteo unicinctus*	0.36	Yes	Yes	Birds/mammals	NA/SA
Ferruginous hawk	*Buteo regalis*	0.49	Yes	Yes	Birds/mammals	NA
Golden eagle	*Aquila chrysaetos*	0.67	Yes	Yes	Birds/mammals	NA/Eur/As
Wedge-tailed eagle	*A. audax*	0.68	Yes	Yes	Birds/mammals/reptiles	Aust
Tawny eagle	*A. rapax*	0.53	Yes	Yes	Catholic	Af/As
Steppe eagle	*A. nipalensis*	0.57	Yes	Yes	Catholic	Eur/As
Lesser spotted eagle	*A. pomerina*	0.43	Yes	No	Birds/mammals	Eur/As
Bonelli's eagle	*Hieraaetus fasciatus*	0.62	Yes	No	Birds/mammals	Eur/Af
Booted eagle	*Hieraaetus pennatus*	0.36	Yes	Yes	Birds/mammals/reptiles	Aust/Eur/Af
Bald eagle	*Haliaeetus leucocephalus*	0.60	Yes	Yes	Carrion	NA/SA
Turkey vulture	*Cathartes aura*	0.48	Yes	Yes	Carrion	NA/SA

The rehabilitator must be very aware that hunting is not simply a matter of going out and killing something, and that the two components of hunting, search and attack, are inextricable. There is no point in releasing a bird that can locate but not catch food, nor in releasing a bird that is able to capture prey, but fails to find it due to inexperience in searching. In the context of rehabilitation, the raptor under care must be rehabilitated in such a way as to ensure that it is capable of carrying out a full range of search and attack methods specific to the prey species. The falconer, too, must be aware of what constitutes a search and attack strategy and how this is to be employed in the hunting field. The zookeeper who is trying to demonstrate a raptor's skills must also be keenly aware of the bird's abilities and limitations if he is to effectively demonstrate the raptor's natural flight behaviors.

1.1.2 Search strategies

Searching for food occupies a good portion of every wild raptor's day; the actual attack, when it does come, may last only a few seconds, or it may culminate in a complex series of feint attacks, stoops, tail-chases, or glide attacks.

Raptors use a number of search strategies.

Perch and search, or still-hunting, typically involves long periods of perching, during which the bird searches the ground directly below, or immediately surrounding, the chosen perch. In the case of a red-tailed hawk, brown falcon, or European kestrel, the attack may be a simple glide down from the perch. Other species, such as peregrines, prairie falcons, and gyrfalcons, may still search from a perch, but use a fast direct attack at their prey, or a fast direct attack mixed with a series of short, shallow stoops followed by a tail-chase.

Listening is another method of searching for prey, often in combination with the perch and search method. In many instances, the raptor will be listening as well as looking, and when prey has been detected, the hunt progresses with a subtle stalk during which the raptor changes perches frequently until it finally comes into visual contact with its target. The raptor may then simply tail-chase its prey until it is caught, or grab it under the snow, as some large owls do when they are hunting rodents during winter.

Figure 1.1.2a   Simple glide attack.

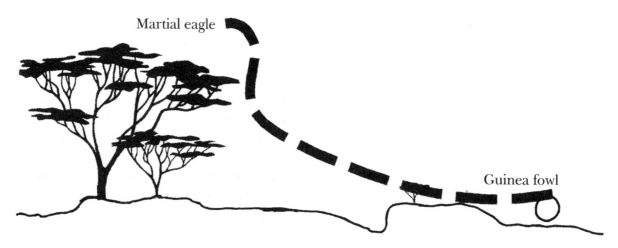

Figure 1.1.2b Typical long distance glide attack by a Martial eagle in Africa.

Soaring is typically used by many raptorial birds as a method of searching for prey. Large eagles, falcons, buzzards, and vultures will soar, weather conditions allowing, in an attempt to locate potential prey. The attack method used from a soaring position varies from a sudden, outright stoop to a long-angled glide.

Prospecting is a method of search that is opportunistic, and involves fast, contour-hugging flight or agile flight through tree cover. This technique is usually used by fast-flying, attacking raptors such as the bird-eating species of falcons and hawks.

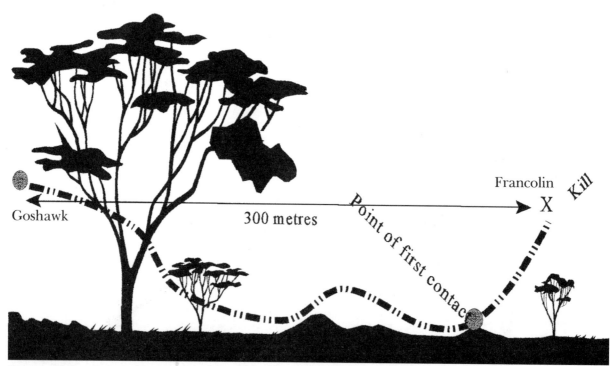

Figure 1.1.2c Prospecting strategy. Black sparrowhawk attacks a francolin.

Quartering is a slow-flying, low altitude method of search typically employed by raptors with a low wing-loading, like harriers, short-eared owls, swallow-tailed kites, and black kites. In quartering, the raptor will meander across grassland, occasionally checking the ground below either by doubling back or by employing a brief hover.

Hovering is the last obvious search strategy. It is thought to have evolved as a method of search in areas where perches are not available, so that the hover becomes, in effect, an aerial perch and search method, followed by a simple drop onto the prey. Many species will briefly hover and then drop suddenly. Harriers will check and hover very briefly while quartering a field if prey is heard below them or if a movement catches their attention. Ospreys, prairie falcons, black falcons, lanner falcons, and brown falcons can all hover for very short periods, but only kestrels and black-shouldered kites are able to sustain hovering for longer periods, sometimes up to ten minutes at a time.

While searching for food is a hard-wired or instinctive behavior, the various attack strategies often need to be perfected through prac-

tice. Many juvenile raptors are simply unable to successfully capture their prey. This may account for the comparatively large numbers of attackers that are brought in for treatment in both the Northern and Southern hemispheres, usually suffering from starvation.

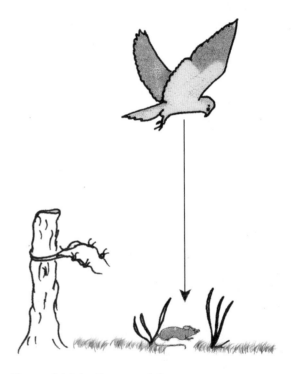

Figure 1.1.2d   Hover and drop.

Table 1.1.2 Search strategies by species.

Species	Listening	Hovering	Soaring	Prospecting	Quartering	Still hunting
Gyrfalcon			Yes	Yes		Yes
Peregrine	Yes		Yes	Yes		Yes
Saker falcon	Yes		Yes	Yes	Yes	Yes
Lanner falcon	Yes	Yes	Yes	Yes		Yes
Aplomado falcon	Yes		Yes	Yes		Yes
Black falcon		Yes	Yes	Yes	Yes	Yes
Brown falcon	Yes	Yes	Yes	Yes	Yes	Yes
Taita falcon			Yes			Yes
Sooty falcon			Yes	Yes		Yes
Eleanora's falcon			Yes	Yes		Yes
Laughing falcon	Yes			Yes		Yes
New Zealand falcon	Yes		Yes	Yes		Yes

Species	Listening	Hovering	Soaring	Prospecting	Quartering	Still hunting
American Kestrel	Yes	Yes	Yes		Yes	Yes
European Kestrel	Yes	Yes	Yes		Yes	Yes
Grey kestrel		Yes	Yes		Yes	Yes
Mauritius kestrel	Yes				Yes	Yes
Merlin			Yes	Yes		Yes
Little falcon			Yes	Yes		Yes
European hobby			Yes	Yes		Yes
Oriental hobby			Yes	Yes		Yes
Red-necked falcon			Yes	Yes		Yes
Harris hawk			Yes	Yes		Yes
Red-tailed hawk			Yes	Yes	Yes	Yes
Broad-winged hawk			Yes	Yes	Yes	Yes
Ferruginous hawk			Yes	Yes	Yes	Yes
Red-shouldered hawk			Yes	Yes	Yes	Yes
Grasshopper buzzard		Yes	Yes		Yes	Yes
White-eyed buzzard			Yes		Yes	Yes
Crane hawk			Yes		Yes	Yes
Gymnogene			Yes		Yes	Yes
Lizard buzzard	Yes		Yes		Yes	Yes
Black kite		Yes	Yes		Yes	Yes
Yellow-billed kite		Yes	Yes		Yes	Yes
Red kite			Yes		Yes	Yes
Gray-headed kite	Yes		Yes		Yes	Yes
Hook-billed kite			Yes		Yes	Yes
European honey buzzard	Yes		Yes		Yes	Yes
American swallow-tailed kite		Yes	Yes		Yes	Yes
Bat hawk			Yes	Yes	Yes	Yes
Black-shouldered kite		Yes	Yes		Yes	Yes
Letter-winged kite		Yes	Yes		Yes	Yes
Snail kite			Yes		Yes	Yes
Mississippi kite			Yes		Yes	Yes
Square-tailed kite	Yes		Yes		Yes	Yes
Whistling kite			Yes		Yes	Yes
Brahminy kite			Yes		Yes	Yes
White-bellied fish-eagle			Yes		Yes	Yes
Steller's sea-eagle			Yes		Yes	Yes
Bald eagle			Yes		Yes	Yes
African fish-eagle			Yes		Yes	Yes
Palm-nut vulture			Yes		Yes	Yes
Egyptian vulture			Yes		Yes	Yes
Hooded vulture	Yes		Yes		Yes	Yes
White-headed vulture			Yes		Yes	Yes
Lappet-faced vulture			Yes		Yes	Yes

Species	Listening	Hovering	Soaring	Prospecting	Quartering	Still hunting
White-backed vulture			Yes		Yes	Yes
Cape vulture			Yes		Yes	Yes
Short-toed eagle		Yes	Yes		Yes	Yes
Banded snake-eagle		Yes	Yes		Yes	Yes
Madagascar serpent-eagle	Yes		Yes		Yes	Yes
Bateleur		Yes	Yes		Yes	Yes
Brown snake-eagle		Yes	Yes		Yes	Yes
African marsh-harrier	Yes	Yes	Yes		Yes	Yes
Swamp harrier	Yes	Yes	Yes		Yes	Yes
Northern harrier	Yes	Yes	Yes		Yes	Yes
Pallid harrier	Yes	Yes	Yes		Yes	Yes
Black harrier	Yes	Yes	Yes		Yes	Yes
Dark chanting goshawk	Yes		Yes		Yes	Yes
Pale chanting goshawk	Yes		Yes		Yes	Yes
Gabar goshawk	Yes		Yes	Yes		Yes
Crested goshawk	Yes		Yes	Yes		Yes
African goshawk	Yes		Yes	Yes		Yes
Northern goshawk	Yes		Yes	Yes		Yes
Doria's goshawk	Yes		Yes	Yes		Yes
Red goshawk			Yes	Yes		Yes
Shikra	Yes			Yes		Yes
Cooper's hawk	Yes		Yes	Yes		Yes
Brown goshawk	Yes		Yes	Yes		Yes
Gray goshawk	Yes		Yes	Yes		Yes
Black-mantled goshawk	Yes		Yes	Yes		Yes
Sharp-shinned hawk	Yes		Yes	Yes		Yes
Little sparrowhawk	Yes		Yes	Yes		Yes
European sparrowhawk	Yes		Yes	Yes		Yes
Ovampo sparrowhawk	Yes		Yes	Yes		Yes
Collared sparrowhawk	Yes		Yes	Yes		Yes
Lesser spotted eagle			Yes	Yes	Yes	Yes
Greater spotted eagle			Yes	Yes	Yes	Yes
Tawny eagle			Yes	Yes	Yes	Yes
Verreaux's eagle			Yes		Yes	Yes
Golden eagle			Yes		Yes	Yes
Imperial eagle			Yes		Yes	Yes
Steppe eagle			Yes	Yes		Yes
Wedge-tailed eagle	Yes		Yes	Yes	Yes	Yes
Gurney's eagle	Yes		Yes	Yes		Yes
Bonelli's eagle			Yes	Yes		Yes
African hawk-eagle			Yes	Yes		Yes
Ayre's hawk-eagle			Yes	Yes		Yes
Little eagle			Yes	Yes	Yes	Yes
Martial eagle			Yes			Yes

Species	Listening	Hovering	Soaring	Prospecting	Quartering	Still hunting
Crowned eagle	Yes		Yes	Yes		Yes
Mountain hawk-eagle	Yes			Yes		Yes
Blyth's hawk-eagle	Yes			Yes		Yes
Cassin's hawk-eagle	Yes		Yes	Yes		Yes
Ornate hawk-eagle	Yes			Yes		Yes
Booted eagle			Yes	Yes	Yes	Yes
Secretary bird			Yes		Yes	Yes
Osprey		Yes	Yes		Yes	Yes
Barn owl	Yes	Yes			Yes	Yes
Grass owl	Yes	Yes			Yes	Yes
Marsh owl	Yes	Yes			Yes	Yes
Great horned owl	Yes				Yes	Yes
Giant eagle-owl	Yes				Yes	Yes
Spotted eagle-owl	Yes				Yes	Yes
Snowy owl	Yes				Yes	Yes
Wood owl	Yes				Yes	Yes
Tawny owl	Yes				Yes	Yes
White-faced owl	Yes				Yes	Yes
Spotted owl	Yes				Yes	Yes
Little owl	Yes				Yes	Yes
Pearl-spotted owl	Yes			Yes		Yes
Pel's fishing-owl	Yes				Yes	Yes
Powerful owl	Yes				Yes	Yes
Barking owl	Yes			Yes		Yes
Boobook owl	Yes					Yes

1.1.3 Attack strategies

Methods of attacking prey may be either simple or very complex, and the initial attack sequence may change mid-stream by being totally abandoned or altered to suit the circumstances. Many of these changes are subtle, and to the casual onlooker, the method of attack may never seem to change at all. Certain attack methods are very strenuous in terms of the amount of energy expended during the attack. The amount of work involved in successfully completing the attack and capture sequence may increase depending on the type of prey selected. For example, a saker falcon or a peregrine works much harder when capturing a duck than does a buzzard when capturing a vole.

Hover and drop is a method employed by many of the world's kestrels, and also by the *Elanus* kites. In many ways this may be considered a search strategy as well as being an attack method. The attack is simple and invariably comprises either a sudden drop onto prey or a measured series of declines followed by a sudden drop. With each decline the bird will check the prey's position before undertaking another short descent. When the prey's exact location is finally verified, the bird will drop with its legs extended.

Stooping is a classic attack strategy. The stoop is a dive carried out with the wings totally or partially closed. The stoop may serve as the primary attack method or as a sec-

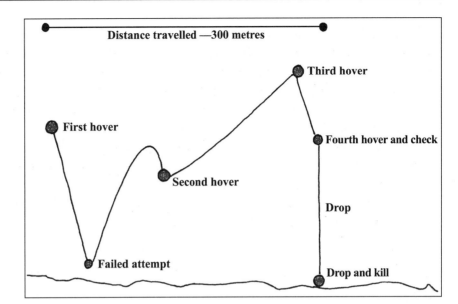

**Figure 1.1.3a
Hover and stoop strategy.**

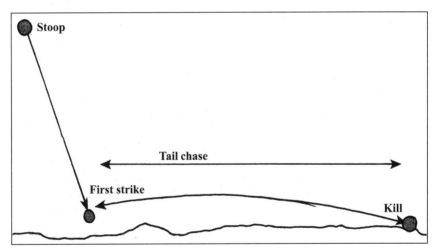

**Figure 1.1.3b
Falcon stoop and subsequent
tail chase.**

ondary method. Prey may be struck in the air and killed outright, or merely collected alive and carried to a perch to be killed. Falcons and some of the smaller hawk eagles use this method of attack. The prey is first located during a soar or through a perch and search session. When attacking from a perch, the raptor will often fly upward in order to gain height to facilitate the stoop.

Tail-chasing, which involves the direct pursuit of prey, is a method used by many Accipiters; goshawks and sparrowhawks are wonderful sprinters, and the tail-chase often results from a perch and search session. The prey is sometimes ambushed and caught unawares after a short sprint; at other times, the chase may be prolonged. Rough-legged hawks and golden eagles often successfully employ long tail-chases. This method is also employed by the larger falcons, such as the peregrine, gyrfalcon, and saker. These species are very adept at long drawn out tail-chases. Prey is either caught and killed in the air or brought to the ground and dispatched before being carried to a feeding perch or to the nest. Tail-chasing can ensue from a soaring position or a perch or after prospecting, and may be combined with a series of short stoops.

The **glide attack** can be confusing to define. In some cases the search will start from a perch and the raptor will locate prey, which could be a small rodent, and then simply glide down to kill it. The process is methodical and straight forward. This mode of attack is often used by buzzards. The glide attack changes if the prey, particularly a rabbit or a bird, moves away suddenly. The glide will immediately change to a sprint, then a tail-chase, usually ending with a short series of stoops.

Golden eagles often start a long-angled glide from a soaring position and catch their prey without resorting to a tail-chase. I have watched tawny eagles do the same, only to change their attack when their target sees them and takes evasive action. In large and small bird-eating falcons, the initial approach may be undetected, but alarm calls from other birds invariably cause panic and the glide attack must then be modified accordingly.

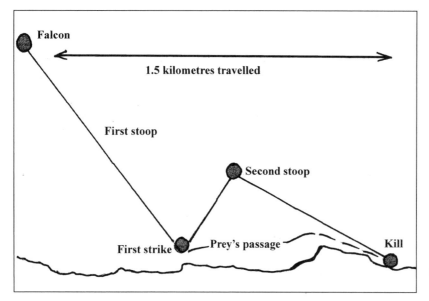

Figure 1.1.3c Falcon attack.

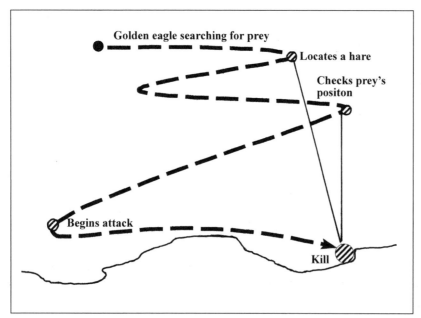

Figure 1.1.3d
Golden eagle's attack strategy.

Table 1.1.3 Attack strategies by species.

Species	Hover/drop	Stoop	Tail-chase	Glide attack	Fast glide	Stalking
Prairie falcon	Yes	Yes	Yes	Yes	Yes	No
Gyrfalcon	No	Yes	Yes	Yes	Yes	No
Saker falcon	Yes	Yes	Yes	Yes	Yes	No
Red-necked falcon	No	Yes	Yes	Yes	Yes	No
African hobby	No	Yes	Yes	Yes	Yes	No
Oriental hobby	No	Yes	Yes	Yes	Yes	No
American kestrel	Yes	Yes	Yes	Yes	Yes	No
Sooty falcon	No	Yes	Yes	Yes	Yes	No
Harrier hawk	No	No	Yes	Yes	No	Yes
Lizard buzzard	No	No	Yes	Yes	Yes	No
Snake eagle	Yes	No	No	Yes	Yes	No
Bateleur	No	Yes	Yes	Yes	Yes	No
Sparrowhawk	No	No	Yes	Yes	Yes	No

1.1.4 Hunt success

The more experience the raptor gains in using a variety of search and attack strategies, the more successful a hunter it will be, which in turn increases its chances of reaching adulthood and potentially breeding. Juvenile mortality is often attributed to a lack of success in foraging, which is generally due to inexperience. A young raptor has the innate ability to carry out a hunt from start to finish using basic foraging strategies, but only with experience will it learn how to vary methods and select suitable prey. Effective prey selection is crucial for survival; juveniles can literally starve to death in a habitat that, to our eyes, is teeming with potential meals. This has significant ramifications when dealing with starving juvenile raptors brought in for care. Parasite burdens or other problems aside, however, the primary cause for starvation among young raptors is invariably a simple lack of experience in selecting or catching prey.

Field studies have consistently indicated that the availability of prey, as well as its accessibility, governs predator populations. The larger the prey base, the greater the existing opportunities. Conversely, a smaller prey base results in increased competition. In addition, the foraging ability of some species can be inhibited by environmental factors. Long, dense grass growth, for example, will ultimately shut out kestrels, as the millions of mice and crickets it harbors become virtually inaccessible. On the other hand, buzzards or harriers fare better under these conditions. Many rehabilitators, by examining their past records, will discover that the appearance of raptor species presented for care and treatment can often be directly linked to the availability and accessibility of the prey population for those species. The experienced rehabilitator, by noting certain environmental circumstances, should be able to predict which raptor species will be showing up in larger numbers.

1.2 WILD DIET

In much the same way as some prey species have habitat overlaps and even dietary overlaps, many raptors overlap in their prey preferences. While it is easy to say that peregrines only eat birds or that the snail kite only eats snails, there are occasions when these two "specialized" species will break the mold and eat other prey items. Raptors are opportunistic and very rarely pass up the chance for a free meal. Habitat variations may also alter prey preferences. Peregrines are perhaps the best example of this; some subspecies rely heavily upon pigeons, some on passerines, and others on seabirds.

There are, however, simple physical attributes to consider. Foot size, toe and tarsus length, wing-loading, and tail length still serve to govern foraging and attack strategies which, as noted earlier, lead to the classification of a raptor as a searcher or attacker. Knowing what a raptor feeds upon in the wild and then looking at how it captures its prey will help in developing rehabilitation and exercise protocols, as well as aid in formulating a flight demonstration. For falconers, this knowledge is vital to selecting the correct raptor for a specific prey in the particular habitat it which it is to be flown.

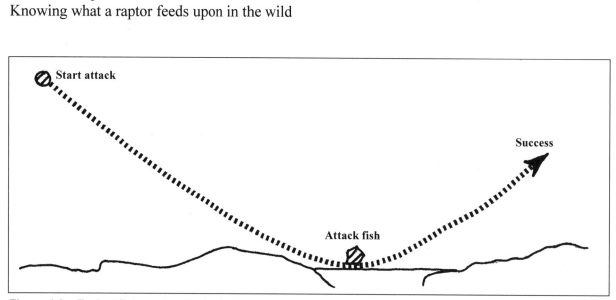

Figure 1.2   Typical fish eagle attack strategy.

Start attack

Attack fish

Success

CHAPTER TWO
THE INJURED RAPTOR

2.1 SOURCE OF BIRDS FOR REHABILITATION

2.1.1 Overview

Raptors may require rehabilitation for many reasons. For example, a fledgling might be injured in a fall from the nest, or a bird may be wounded during an escape from a predator. Some birds will not have developed the skills to effectively compete and as a result may become weak from starvation and therefore susceptible to infection. Other injuries, however, are the direct result of increased urbanization and agricultural development. Many birds are injured on roads, by fences, by power lines, or by other hazards that are part of an urban or suburban environment.

Some species are more predisposed to this type of "unnatural" injury than others. Raptors classified as attackers, such as bird-eating falcons and accipiters, are more likely to suffer from direct collisions with fences, windows, and power lines. Larger raptors that soar or sit around farmland are more likely to be shot by people defending their livestock.

Those species of raptors classified as searchers are more likely to be struck by vehicles. They expose themselves to injury as they forage along major roads, highways, or quiet country lanes, having been attracted by the insects and small rodents in the grassy verges. The incidence of road-strikes has increased with the placement of fence and power posts that serve as convenient perches. Finally, there are always fledglings that are found orphaned, or juveniles found starving, or young birds that have become caught in chicken coops or pigeon lofts. These injured or rescued raptors are regularly handed over to rehabilitation centers, local zoos, or falconers.

2.1.2 Rescuing the injured raptor

Any bird of prey which can be picked up or handled freely has a problem. It is either injured or starving, or both, unless of course it has been hand-reared. Always assume injury until a full physical examination has proven otherwise. If a bird is healthy, any attempt to restrain it will normally produce an escape

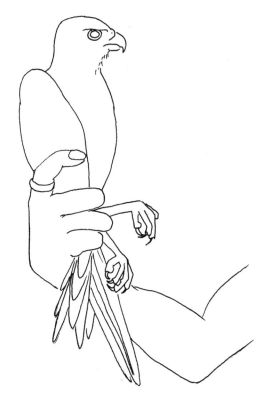

Figure 2.1.2a Restraining a small falcon.

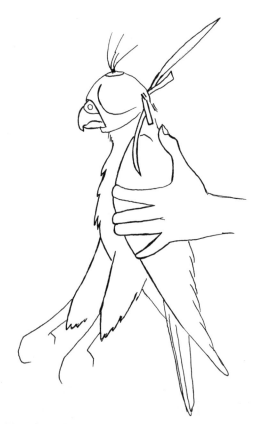

Figure 2.1.2b Restraining a large falcon.

response. Often, an effective response is prevented by an injury which is subtle and difficult to detect, such as a fracture in the shoulder. If the bird is seriously damaged, there may be no response at all. For these reasons, all birds of prey which are presented for rehabilitation must be taken to a veterinarian for evaluation. There should be no exceptions to this rule.

Many of the problems associated with raptor rescue and the bird's recovery revolve around inexperience. We see many birds which have been held for periods ranging from a week up to a month by amateur but well-meaning care-givers who simply do not realize the extent of the bird's injuries. When these birds are finally presented to the rehabilitation center, the fractured bones have often healed abnormally, or a damaged piece of soft tissue has become infected. What may have been a treatable problem initially is now totally unsalvageable. Re-breaking old fractures and attempting to repair them is not possible in birds due to the brittle nature of their bones. Often the only remaining option is euthanasia.

Immobilizing the bird should be the first priority, as injured raptors are invariably frightened and will defend themselves in any way they can. Throwing a towel or blanket over the bird will help, for even if the raptor is a large eagle, such a covering will give the rescuer enough time to restrain the legs and wings. Raptors can inflict painful bites, but their talons can do more damage, so make sure the feet are properly restrained.

Initial examination should take place as soon as possible. It is vital that the extent of the injury be ascertained quickly, although there will be occasions when the bird will need time to settle down before being subjected to the extra stress of being put under a general anaesthetic. Experienced rescuers may be able to assess an injured raptor's future at the point of capture. Severe fractures which are irreparable or which will ultimately inhibit normal flight can be diagnosed and appropriate action, such as euthanasia, taken.

2.1.3 Transportation of injured raptors

Injured wild birds of prey are likely to be stressed, and conceivably in shock. They should be handled as little as possible, and kept in a warm, quiet, dark area while transportation is being organized.

Transport containers must be secure and clean. Custom-made boxes designed for transporting birds of prey are obviously ideal, but failing that, one can use a pet-carrier or even a heavy-duty cardboard box. The bird should not be transported in a bag or hessian sack as this will ruin its feathers. Care must be taken to ensure that feathers are not damaged, as this could result in an unnecessary delay in the scheduled release date of the bird, possibly by as much as twelve months or more if a molt is required to replace the damaged feathers. The bird should be kept quiet during transportation. It should never be left unattended in a vehicle or placed in the trunk of a car.

No food should be offered prior to examination by the veterinarian, as it is likely that he or she will anaesthetize the bird in order to assess its condition and the extent of its injuries. A crop full of food may be regurgitated during anaesthesia, resulting in possible asphyxiation. Water can be offered in a bowl which cannot be tipped over; small dog water bowls are ideal for this purpose.

If transportation to a veterinarian is delayed, a preliminary check for obvious injuries can be made.

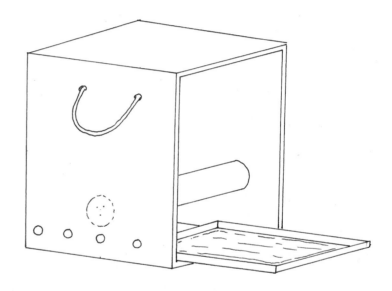

Figure 2.1.3a Transport box.

Figure 2.1.3b Transport box with perch for gripping — suitable for small raptors.

2.1.4 Checking for obvious injuries

❑ A. The first step is to locate the injury. If no injury is visible, take into account where the bird was when found. An injured bird found along a highway was probably struck by an automobile. A bird found beneath a window may have flown into the glass.

❑ B. Ascertain and record the species, sex, and age of the bird.

❑ C. Assess and record the bird's general condition. The body weight and the condition of the sternum will prove useful in this regard. A very pronounced breast bone will indicate malnourishment. Having confirmed the bird's sex and species will further assist you in gauging its condition.

❑ D. Seek veterinary help as soon as possible if the initial examination was not performed by a qualified veterinarian or technician.

2.1.5 What should one look for?

❑ A. Fractures of any bone and/or dislocations of any joint.

❑ B. Foot infection, such as bumblefoot.

❑ C. Infections in the mouth.

❑ D. Imperfect vision.

❑ E. Broken feathers.

❑ F. Signs of emaciation.

After the bird has been removed from the transport box, the next step is to establish the nature and severity of its injury. If the bird has been taken to a vet, the examination can be carried out under general anaesthetic. If the relevant details have been recorded prior to the examination, the veterinarian will have valuable information with which to work.

2.1.6 The proper procedure for examining the injured raptor

❑ A. Restrain the bird. Hold its wings together and restrain its feet.

❑ B. Hold it down on a cushion.

❑ C. Examine both wings, one at a time, by gently extending them. Feel the joints and check for swelling, particularly in the shoulders, elbows, and carpal joints.

❑ D. Check for feather damage on each wing and the tail.

❑ E. Check the feet and legs for swelling, abrasions, or abscesses.

❑ F. Check the bird's head, mouth, and eyes. Examine the beak for cracks. Look for blood in the mouth and obstructions in the throat, or any signs of ulcerations or lesions.

The results of this initial examination will dictate the next course of action. Loose limbs or protruding bones are easily diagnosed. If the bird seems uncoordinated, it is likely that some head trauma exists. At this point, the area where the bird was found may provide a clue toward confirmation of the diagnosis. Collision with vehicles or windows is a common occurrence with some species. Severe bleeding can be controlled by applying digital pressure to the site, or by using a temporary bandage. Sticky bandages such as Elastoplast must not be used, as the glue will damage the feathers. A self-adhering bandage such as Vetrap, which uses a similar principle to velcro, is ideal. A severely drooping wing can be temporarily bandaged to the body to prevent further damage to the internal musculature and bones, the wings, or the feathers. Disinfectants such as Mercurochrome should not be used, as they will make examination more difficult, damage the feathers, and if used in large amounts, may chill the bird and possibly exacerbate any existing shock.

2.1.7 Establishing sex, age, and species

Determining the species, sex, and age of a bird is also important, as it will be impossible to properly assess the bird's general condition unless one knows precisely what species he is dealing with. In raptors, males are generally smaller than females, and juveniles have a different plumage. A good field guide will be of great assistance when trying to establish which species of raptor has been presented for rehabilitation.

2.1.8 Ascertaining body condition

The sternum or breast bone will be pronounced if the raptor is malnourished, a fact which will be confirmed when the patient is weighed and checked against the correct weight range for its species, sex, and age.

However, one must be very careful about using weight charts from field guides, as one never knows the condition of the birds that were weighed, and even falconers who trap birds rarely record their exact condition, e.g., one has a variation in weights which can range from 490–710 grams for male Australian peregrine falcons.

Record the color of the injured or orphaned bird's feces. This is another good indication of its general condition. Green fecal matter is a sure sign that the gut is totally empty and an absence of fecal matter is even worse—there is nothing in the gut to pass as waste material.

If one is new to dealing with raptors, with limited experience in the falconry, rehabilitation, or demonstration fields, then finding a good veterinarian who is familiar with raptors is an essential starting point. Getting in touch with raptor breeders, falconers, and other experienced rehabilitators is equally vital.

2.2 HOUSING THE INJURED RAPTOR

2.2.1 Overview

Any sick or injured animal is potentially carrying a disease that is transmissible to other captive stock, so quarantine protocols must be established and strictly followed, even in a small rehabilitation center, such as a backyard operation. Every effort must be taken to prevent the possibility of infecting additional animals with some obscure parasite or disease.

Ideally, one should have three basic enclosure types, each catering to a specific period in the injured raptor's recovery. The dimensions of each enclosure vary from institute to institute, and the measurements provided in table 2.2.5 represent a combination from various sources. The initial confinement enclosure should facilitate easy capture or restraint of the patient and allow heating if necessary. Extremely sick birds can be kept in smaller boxes until their condition has stabilized. In most cases, I use the following three enclosure types described.

2.2.2 Initial care enclosures

Commercially made, heavy-duty plastic boxes are easily cleaned and disinfected, and can be moved around with the minimum of work. These boxes are not suitable, however, for large species such as eagles or large kites, falcons, and hawks, as the doors are too small. Custom-made wooden boxes that have been surface-sealed to make them waterproof are ideal. Hygiene is vital and the water-proofed wooden boxes can be washed and disinfected with no detrimental effects to the wood.

When is it safe to move the raptor into a bigger enclosure?

- When injuries have stabilized.
- When the bird is feeding voluntarily and is gaining weight.
- When, after suffering from head trauma, the bird has regained its coordination.

In most instances, a confinement of one to five days in the initial care enclosure is sufficient to see the bird through the critical period.

2.2.3 Secondary care enclosures

These are larger enclosures with a window at one end to provide natural light. The floors should be of cleanable, sealed concrete covered with astroturf carpets to prevent the possibility of further injury to the bird.

The placement, number, and type of perches will depend upon the individual occupant and its mobility. Traditionally, flat blocks are used for falcons and branches for other birds of prey, but both types could be provided. Smooth branches should not be used for perches, as these invariably cause calluses and foot sores. Perches must be covered with astroturf, hemp rope, or a similar rough material to provide a textured surface. The bird's talons should never be able to completely encircle the perch or branch. Insufficient perch diameter places pressure on the ball of the foot, which may lead to other complications. The sharp talons can puncture the foot resulting in infection. It is important to remember that while in the wild the bird can choose where to perch, in the enclosure it can only use what has been provided. It is also necessary for the bird to have access to water. This type of sealed enclosure is ideal for nervous species, such as goshawks. In situations where the injury to the raptor has been minor, release can be facilitated from this type of enclosure as long as the bird has met all the pre-release requirements (see section 2.4).

2.2.4 Tertiary care enclosures

The bigger these enclosures are, the better. They must offer the raptor the opportunity of self-exercise in an environment that is not

Table 2.2.4 Enclosure dimensions in meters

Species	Initial						Secondary	Tertiary
Eagles	1	x	1	x	1		2 x 2 x 2	25 x 5 x 5
Vultures	1	x	1	x	1		2 x 3 x 2	25 x 5 x 5
Large falcons	1	x	1	x	1		2 x 2 x 2	25 x 5 x 5
Small falcons	.5	x	.5	x	.5		2 x 2 x 2	25 x 5 x 5
Small hawks	.5	x	.5	x	.5		2 x 2 x 2	25 x 5 x 5
Large hawks	1	x	1	x	1		2 x 2 x 2	25 x 5 x 5
Buzzards	1	x	1	x	1		2 x 2 x 2	25 x 5 x 5
Small owls	1	x	1	x	1		2 x 2 x 2	10 x 4 x 3
Large owls	1	x	1	x	1		2 x 2 x 2	25 x 5 x 5

stressful. Open plan flight aviaries constructed from loosely hung nylon mesh are preferable to wire mesh enclosures. Many organizations use vertical slatted enclosures, with a partially sealed roof. For the wildlife rescuer who is self-funded, this type of enclosure can be expensive, particularly if the recommended dimensions are followed. Nylon mesh is cheaper and serves the same purpose, but care must be taken to make the lower part of the enclosure predator proof.

If vegetation is to be added to the enclosure, make sure that fast-growing trees are kept pruned and flight paths within the aviary kept clear. I feel that this type of enclosure is perfect for the rehabilitation of a wide range of species–it can be planted to create secluded areas and shelter from rain, wind, and sun. A heavy mulch substrate will attract invertebrate life, providing small raptor species like kestrels an opportunity to forage naturally.

2.2.5 Perches

The odd log in an aviary is not necessarily the ideal perching arrangement. Factors such as the bird's size, the size of its feet, and its ability to fly competently should determine the number of perches and the height at which they are placed. Natural branches are obviously ideal, but it is equally as important to offer the bird a variety of perches with different surface textures and diameters, similar to those found in its wild environment. Covering

even the natural perches with strips of coco-fiber matting from old door mats, or with astroturf, and ensuring that the bird's talons cannot encircle the perch, will prevent the development of foot complaints.

Newly introduced raptors that are still unable to fly comfortably will not be able to reach high perches unless "runners" are placed up to them. Even in these situations it is wise not to place the perches too high off the ground. An eagle that has just been introduced to a large enclosure and is still a bit stiff, can land very badly and possibly sustain further injury if it takes off from a height. High perches are always sought after the birds have recovered sufficiently to use them, so make these comfortable and sheltered from the elements.

2.2.6 Water access

Raptors do drink and bathe, so it is important to supply a pond for this purpose. A dish with steep sides is not always suitable. A fiberglass pool or a permanent concrete pond of no more than 12 in. (300 mm) deep at the deepest point would suit a variety of raptors. The bird should be able to wade in to a depth where it feels comfortable–about 4 in. (100 mm) of water for small falcons, but as eagles and vultures require more, make the pond versatile by using a design that has a varying depth of 4–12 in. (100–300 mm).

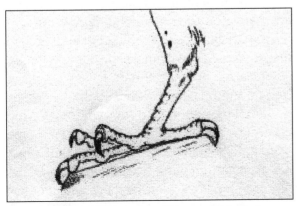

Figure 2.2.5a A flat surface for a perch is not healthy during long periods of inactivity.

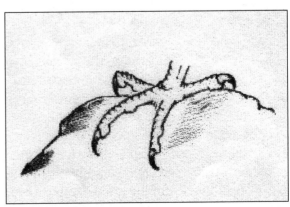

Figure 2.2.5b A perch surface that has a variable texture is by far more comfortable.

2.3 ENCLOSURE CONSTRUCTION

2.3.1 Materials

Using wire mesh in the construction of any rehabilitation aviary is a recipe for disaster. Nervous, fast-flying hawks, if placed in an aviary made from wire mesh, will quickly damage feathers and ceres. Additionally, existing problems such as a lack of basic flight competence will be exacerbated. In short, wire mesh can kill raptors.

The options in terms of what to use when building a flight aviary are limited. Loosely hung nylon mesh, or wooden slats placed vertically, will limit or eliminate any potential damage to the bird within the aviary. It is possible to construct large, 160 ft. (50 m) aviaries using 1 in. (24 mm) nylon mesh, and then build or place shelters within the enclosure.

2.3.2 Predator proofing

Raptors are not immune to attack by other predators. Cats, dogs, coyotes, raccoons, genets, baboons, and large reptiles will not pass up the chance to eat a raptor that is obviously confined. Other raptors, such as the large owls, will also kill and eat smaller captive raptors. Having secure and sheltered areas in the aviary will assist in keeping the cage-bound bird out of reach from marauding eagle-owls or great horned owls, which is another reason for not placing the perches too close to a mesh roof or sides.

For protection against mammalian predators, it is important to secure the perimeter of the flight enclosure with a wire mesh fence, and to bury at least 24 in. (600 mm) of mesh under the ground. This really should be done even if the aviary is made up of vertical slats. Uneaten food left in an aviary will attract other carnivores, therefore careful attention to basic cleanliness is of the utmost importance.

2.3.3 Wind breaks

There can be nothing more miserable for the captive raptor than being left in an aviary open to the elements, without shelter. Wild raptors can choose either to seek shelter when desired, or sit in the rain. Captive raptors should be provided with the same options, allowing them to perch in or out of the rain or sun. Constructing shelters within the aviary is one solution; building half or a quarter of the aviary in the form of a semi-enclosed and roofed-over pen is another. One should take into account the prevailing wind, and situate the aviary in such a position that at least some of the pen is sheltered. The same applies to sunlight. The mid-day sun in some parts of the world is ruthless–providing shade, and the option of seeking shade, is not only wise but humane.

2.3.4 Other considerations and complications

Not all injuries require long term captive management. The less time a raptor spends in captivity the better, for no matter how well one manages injured birds, there is always the risk of causing additional damage. Some raptors do not cope well at all with being confined, and will inevitably damage or break feathers, which will ultimately inhibit flight, especially in the large direct attacking falcons. They are difficult to condition to pen life, and alternative housing and conditioning through falconry techniques are often required. Severe feather damage will make the raptor totally unreleasable until a full molt has taken place. Certain injuries that involve a joint, or joints, in the wing often end up with the wing becoming permanently shortened. This type of complication or extension deficit will affect fast-flying, high wing-loaded birds more than those with a low wing-loading, and this has much to do with hunting and flight style.

The decision to retain a raptor in captivity for rehabilitation will depend upon the time it has to spend recovering from injuries.

a) If a raptor has spent a recovery time for minor injuries of less than 21 days in captivity and has within that time fully recovered from any injury, it can be released immediately, provided it has met all the pre-release checks (section 2.4.9).

b) If a raptor has spent more than 21 days in captivity, but less than 30 days, and has recovered from any injuries, it can be liberated, but care should be taken when making this decision. Factors which should be taken into account include the bird's age and species, its foraging experience, and its ability to perform the pertinent hunting strategies.

c) If a raptor has spent more than 30 days in captivity, its flight ability should be assessed in an aviary. Flight training may be necessary.

2.4 CHOOSING THE RIGHT REHABILITATION METHOD

Choosing the correct method of rehabilitation is crucial for any rehabilitator. In order to make the proper decision, the rehabilitator should understand the foraging and attacking strategies of individual species of raptors. Refer to earlier tables 1.1.2 and 1.1.3 in Chapter 1.

In some cases it is vital that the bird undergoing rehabilitation be allowed to carry out a range of natural foraging strategies. The raptor may need to learn how to forage, and, although assisting a hawk or falcon to kill its prey is acceptable, too much assistance in the search component can be counter-productive. Techniques whereby the hawk is allowed and encouraged to perform the attack component can be misleading as a method of establishing overall foraging competence, unless careful attention is also paid to foraging ability.

Ultimately, the bird should always be assessed on its ability to forage using its own repertoire of techniques; for example a large falcon undergoing rehabilitation may have been successful at still-hunting before it was injured, therefore, it should not be considered deficient, or forced into finding its prey by using one particular strategy, such as a stoop. Once again, let me stress the importance of considering the specific raptor, its species, inate characteristics, sex, age, past life experiences, and the nature of its injury, and then planning a rehabilitation strategy that will achieve the goal of survival.

2.4.1 The small falcons

The small bird-eating falcons can be rehabilitated from an aviary, in much the same way as small falcons that have a more generalist approach to foraging. Large flight pens around 80 ft. (25 m) in length are good for rehabilitation. If the injury is not serious and the falcon has recovered fully within twenty-one days, then immediate release is possible.

There are exceptions to this rule. Some small falcons, such as the merlin, the Australian little falcon, or the red-necked falcon, that have been injured before attaining a reasonable level of foraging proficiency, should be offered a chance to prove their proficiency, either by tame hacking or free flight under controlled conditions. This will allow the rehabilitator to assess both flight competence and total foraging ability, as well as allowing the bird to gain additional experience. Of course, the rehabilitator needs to consider the amount of time he has available and the number of birds he has in care, as well as his access to flying areas, and any local wildlife regulations that might apply. Sometimes aviary exercise, either forced or encouraged, is the only option available.

The loss of an eye will affect the typical attackers more than it will the typical searchers, and critical evaluation will be necessary if the small falcon is one of the former. Remember that the loss of an eye will eliminate all binocular vision. In familiar surroundings this may not be clearly apparent, but in novel hunting situations the bird will be handicapped. Tame hacking or flight training will provide an opportunity to evaluate the bird's performance in unfamiliar surroundings. Kestrels that typically perch and search will be much less handicapped, and their proficiency can be evaluated within a large enclosure. If the enclosure substrate consists of leaf litter or a heavy mulch and is partially open to the elements, kestrels can forage for insects that have been introduced or that occur naturally within the substrate.

Orphans should be hacked in groups. A single orphan may be tame hacked, but ideally it should be passed on to another rehabilitator with birds of a similar age. Traditional hacking is the ideal method of reintroducing uninjured orphans to their natural habitat, i.e., orphans that do not require rehabilitation.

2.4.2 Large falcons

Large falcons are more problematic in terms of choosing viable and effective rehabilitation methods:

a) Juveniles, no history of independence: Tame hack.

b) Juveniles, proven history of independence, recovery within three weeks: Release immediately.
c) Adults, recovery within three weeks: Release immediately.
d) Juveniles, history of independence, long-term injury, compromised flight: Flight training.
e) Adults, history of independence, long-term injury, compromised flight: Flight training or extensive aviary exercise.

Many of the large falcons (weighing between 600–2000 grams) are typical attackers. They have some searching tendencies, particularly within their first year, when they have longer and more pliable primary and tail feathers. Even so, this should not diminish the importance of overall foraging and flight competence.

One of the biggest factors influencing the method of rehabilitation for large, heavy-bodied falcons is time and space. The average peregrine needs a great deal of air space in which to exercise and hunt, a sports oval being the minimum requirement. If, in addition, the bird needs a chance to prove foraging efficiency, then the availability of suitable prey species is another complication. Adult falcons and juveniles that have proven foraging ability can be rehabilitated from a large enclosure and then simply released in the appropriate area at the right time, always taking into account the time of year and whether or not the bird is on passage (migrating).

Falcons or other raptors that are injured during migration, and then subsequently held up because of injury, will be in a difficult position if released six weeks later. In this case it is often worth contacting rehabilitators at the other end of the falcon's migration route and then shipping the bird there for rehabilitation or release. Alternatively, the bird can be held over and then released the following season, but this is generally not a desirable option as the bird will then be out of condition. Any large falcon that is injured and forced to rest for four to five weeks, or longer, ideally should be actively flown using traditional falconry methods or variations thereof. As mentioned previously, time and space can be limiting factors; those who cannot manage the task should give the bird to someone who is willing and capable.

It is also vital to look at the injury and its effects on the bird, and determine what is needed to bring the bird back to normal physical health. The loss of an eye is a serious problem for any large falcon. It is possible to allow some latitude for adult females, but for adult males who are placed under incredible hunting pressures during the breeding season, there can be no latitude when considering release.

Wing extension deficits, or the shortening of a wing as a result of an injury or inadequate treatment, will make release impossible. Missing toes, particularly the hind toe on one or both feet, will also limit hunting efficiency, but this can be evaluated through periods of tame hack. When evaluating a juvenile's hunting proficiency, one must always remember to take into account its age, as it may fail to kill through inexperience, which can be exacerbated by the loss of a digit.

Traditional hacking in the case of orphan sibling groups is a good way of reintroduction to the wild, but the area for hacking must be chosen carefully.

2.4.3 The owls

Owls are comparatively easy to rehabilitate, the only method available being aviary exercise. The large eagle-owls will need to be assessed for full flight capabilities either by forced flight within an enclosure or by using a creance. It is not worth spending time trying to condition owls that are parent-reared. Any form of falconry method or basic positive reinforcement techniques will fail. Aviary exercise is the only option for owls, large or small. Traditional hacking for sibling groups (orphans) is the best method of reintroduction.

2.4.4 The harriers

Harriers are typical searchers and, as their methods are not physically taxing, aviary exercise or creance work will be sufficient for all harrier species. Creance flying is a good method of ascertaining flight competence, but care needs to be taken because harriers have long legs; sudden jerks to halt a flying harrier can result in broken legs.

Any eye damage will need to be assessed, as a missing eye will handicap even a harrier, although not to the same extent as it would a goshawk or a large falcon. Loss of wing extension is also a less severe handicap in the harriers. Due to their low wing-loading, any loss of extension, within reason, can be compensated for rather easily.

Most harriers do not do well in large open aviaries; they tend to avoid perches, preferring to sit on the ground. For this reason it is advisable to ensure that any flight enclosure provides some cover, such as tussocks of grass. Some harriers are migratory, so if any bird is held over for treatment during migration, it should not be released out of season. Sibling groups can be traditionally hacked using a domed wire cage placed on the ground in the appropriate area. The dome can be removed just prior to fledging, and food placed near the artificial nest on a daily basis.

2.4.5 The true hawks

Accipiters are problematic in a captive situation. They are often thought of as being nervous, highly strung, neurotic, and generally unmanageable. Much of their behavior stems from their foraging methods. They are ambush specialists and often spend their days in dense or closed canopy woodlands; being exposed invariably makes them uncomfortable. They have a quick reaction time and will respond to any visual or audio stimulus with a flurry of activity, leading to the assumption that they are nervous and highly strung.

True hawks are sprint specialists and their attack strategies, while appearing to be simple and straightforward, are extremely complicated. The sprint from a perch is triggered either by a movement below or ahead of them, or by watching prey species feeding close by. Search strategies are also complex. Waiting in ambush relies upon a good likelihood that prey will appear, and the site selection for an ambush is far from random, particularly with adult goshawks.

The injured hawk, either juvenile or adult, will need special care in all the treatment phases. Let me stress that any repeated capture and restraint, such as is required when using a forced exercise regime, will invariably result in well-established fear responses. This will make the use of any flight training or falconry methods virtually impossible in the future. The true hawk that needs overall rehabilitation to improve flight ability or fitness is best left in a large "sealed" enclosure, such as a room equipped with shelf perches or wall-mounted bow perches to which the bird is tethered. Flight conditioning along a corridor proves of little value with a hawk, as it will take a long time to condition the bird to repeat the desired behavior. Accipiters do not do well in large, exposed aviaries.

The choices for rehabilitation are simple and should follow the rules set for large falcons:

a) Juveniles, no history of independence: Tame hack.
b) Juveniles, proven history of independence, recovery within three weeks: Release immediately.
c) Adults, recovery within three weeks: Release immediately.
d) Juveniles, history of independence, long-term injury, compromised flight: Flight training.
e) Adults, history of independence, long-term injury, compromised flight: Flight training or extensive aviary exercise.

If the rehabilitator selects flight training/falconry methods and the hawk needs to be assessed for a range of abilities, additional care must be taken. One should make sure that flight training sets out to achieve certain objectives. If the bird needs fitness enhancement, then develop fitness by means of vertical flights or a dragged lure. If the hawk needs time to experiment with foraging, then fly it in an area where there is a good prey base that offers a variety of situations and opportunities. It is vital to observe the bird and then assess its progress. Success is based upon the raptor's ability to forage competently without undue assistance from the rehabilitator. Traditional hacking can also be used with the true hawks, but once again, choose the correct habitat for the placement of the hack box.

2.4.6 The buzzards, or broad-winged hawks

The buzzards comprise a varied group of raptors, extending from the Americas to Asia. They are all searchers, have a varied prey base, and as a result they are quite common and therefore frequently admitted as patients to raptor rehabilitation centers. All methods of rehabilitation work well with the buzzards. They can be flown using falconry methods, but they can also be rehabilitated from large aviaries or conditioned to fly set exercise courses along a corridor. Orphans can be hacked efficiently in sibling groups. The red-tailed hawk, or buzzard, often used by falconers, is a frequent patient at many bird of prey centers. Therefore, if one ends up with a single orphan, it often isn't difficult to find someone who has a group, or at least a falconer who could assist in tame hacking or even flying the bird for the first few months before it is released. Migratory species are more difficult, but once again, it is wise to follow simple rules regarding when and where to release.

2.4.7 The large and small eagles

The golden eagle is probably the best known of the large eagles in Europe, and also occurs in North America, where the bald eagle is better-known and more frequently encountered. Injuries to eagles vary from gunshot wounds to fractures caused by collision, trap wounds, and many more obscure ailments. Poisoning is another comparatively common problem. In Australia, the wedge-tailed eagle is a frequent patient at many small rehabilitation centers. The steppe eagle, tawny eagle, and Wahlberg's eagle are commonly encountered in Africa and Europe. The hawk-eagles (small eagles) are less frequently admitted for treatment or care, but they should be treated like an eagle, even though some small species behave like true hawks.

Most eagles are searchers that are capable of killing large prey items; some are also opportunistic feeders, especially when they are juveniles or sub-adults, or if they live in colder climates, and will scavenge for carrion which provides a good source of food. Bald eagles prefer to feed on the carcasses of fish, game, or cattle, and many golden eagles will feed upon dead deer. Invariably there will be times when carrion is scarce or not available, so competition for food is fierce. Tawny eagles in Africa have to contend with five species of vulture, and at certain times of the year they have to compete with a number of migrant eagles, such as the steppe eagle, small spotted eagle, greater spotted eagle, and the bateleur. An eagle should never be released with the expectation that it can survive on carrion—it must be able to hunt its prey successfully. The exception here are juvenile bald

eagles that only gain adequate flying and hunting skills after a season of haggling over fish carcasses. they must be released at times of abundant food such as fish spawns.

Injuries need to be assessed critically and all factors, such as the bird's age, sex, and the nature of the injury, need to be taken into account before setting and implementing rehabilitation strategies. Eagles are best left in large enclosures, either slatted or constructed from nylon mesh. An eagle needs at least 160 ft. (50 m) of aviary length to fly properly; this is vital if the injury has caused major loss of wing mobility. A bird with minor injuries that have not caused any major loss of fitness or basic flying ability can be left in a smaller enclosure, then flown on a creance for assessment. Flight training eagles is difficult and flight training using falconry methods is time-consuming, but if it is warranted, and one has the time and is dealing with a single eagle or a small number of patients, then by all means these techniques should be employed.

Single orphans (most orphaned eagles are single) are very difficult indeed. Eagles have a long dependency period and tame hacking an orphaned eagle is a long process, as the hack area can only be used for that one bird. Fostering to a wild nest is an option, particularly if the wild pair has a similar aged chick or failed to produce offspring. Traditional hacking is another option, but the effectiveness is often reduced because of the long period of dependency. Tame hacking, despite its drawbacks in terms of time and effort, is by far the best option for orphaned eagles. This method has been widely used in North America to reestablish the bald eagle. However, great care must be taken to ensure that the young eagles do not become accustomed to man and later seek out humans for food.

2.4.8 The vultures

The vultures are the easiest raptors to rehabilitate. Flight competence is the most important requirement for an injured vulture. For this reason, large enclosures are important. Orphaned vultures can be fostered or hacked. Some vultures have a complex social structure and assimilation into wild groups is important for natural development. Hack sites should be placed near areas where wild vultures roost.

2.4.9   Release requirements

Before being returned to the wild, the rehabilitated raptor must meet the following requirements:

a) The bird should be in perfect feather condition, with no broken or missing feathers other than those that have been naturally molted out.

b) The bird should be able to negotiate the full length of the flight pen in level flight regularly without becoming exhausted.

c) The bird must be able to use both legs, and must have perfect vision.

d) The bird must be physically fit and at maximum weight for its species and sex.

e) The bird should not display any behavioral problems, imbalances, shaking, fits, etc.

2.5 REHABILITATION TECHNIQUES

What can one do to rehabilitate a raptor and yet take into account the rehabilitator's personal restrictions, such as time, space and expertise?

Common sense and a knowledge of what is required of the raptor in the wild should answer this question. If one does not have proper facilities available for the bird he is holding, or is for any reason unable to devote the time and energy required to provide adequate care, then the bird in question should be passed on to someone who has the appropriate housing and can make the necessary commitment to its full recovery.

Rehabilitation methods or techniques should be chosen that take into account the bird's sex, age, and species, as well as type of injury and any additional problems that may have ensued. There are dozens of scenarios that could face the rehabilitator, but a logical approach is the best. If one takes a moment to reflect on what he can and cannot do in terms of preparation for release, he will be in a position to make informed decisions before taking action.

Rehabilitation entails more than the basic care and treatment of injuries, followed by release; it implies, and requires, the proper conditioning and preparation of the bird for release after it has been restored to health. One should never forget that a predator must be able to both find and hunt its food efficiently. Life in the wild involves constant risk, and the raptor must be adequately prepared if it is to survive after release. The rehabilitator needs to assess each bird's situation and adopt the most suitable rehabilitation techniques. The following categories may serve as a guide.

2.5.1 Juveniles — dependent

Juveniles that have never reached independence, including nestlings and fledglings that have been injured or orphaned do not have full flight competence and its development will be retarded. On full recovery from an injury, the orphaned raptor will still have to contend with a lack of fitness, lack of total flight ability, and lack of foraging competence.

Objectives: a) Develop flight competence.
b) Develop foraging strategies and hunting technique competence.
c) Develop physical fitness.

2.5.2 Juveniles — some experience

Juveniles that have a history of independence, but due to injury have lost all fitness and flight ability.

Objectives: a) Improve physical fitness.

b) Improve flight competence.
c) Assess foraging ability in the areas of search and attack.

2.5.3 Adults — experienced

Adults that have suffered an injury and have lost basic fitness and flight competence already understand their search and attack strategies.

Objectives: a) Improve physical fitness.
b) Improve flight competence.

2.6 REVIEW OF INJURIES, CONSEQUENCES, AND OPTIONS

Many injuries, if left untreated, will result in the raptor becoming unreleasable; even untreated minor injuries can lead to major complications later. In order to put the rehabilitation process into perspective, it is worth listing all the variables that can complicate the process. In tables 2.6.1 and 2.6.2, some simple injuries and their resultant consequences are outlined. With each injury there is the possibility of complications that can exacerbate the original problem.

Table 2.6.1 Injuries and their consequences (Richard Naisbitt)

Species	Injury/other	Recovery time	Loss of fitness	Loss of flight ability	Rehab Method
Large (bird-eating) falcon					
	Head trauma	10 days	No	No	Aviary exercise
	Soft tissue damage	10 - 21 days	No	Yes	Aviary exercise
	Leg fracture	3 - 6 weeks	Yes	No	Aviary exercise/ Flight training
	Wing fracture	3 - 6 weeks	Yes	Yes	Aviary exercise/ Flight training
	Coracoid fracture	3 - 6 weeks	Yes	Yes	Aviary exercise/ Flight training
	Gross featherdamage	3 - 12 months			Aviary exercise/ Flight training
	Starvation	21 days	No	No	Aviary exercise/ Flight training
	Orphaned	N/A			Hacking/Tame hacking/Fostering

Species	Injury/other	Recovery time	Loss of fitness	Loss of flight ability	Rehab Method
Small (bird eating) falcon					
	Head trauma	10 days	No	No	Aviary exercise
	Soft tissue damage	10 - 21 days	No	No	Aviary exercise
	Leg fracture	3 - 6 weeks	Yes	No	Aviary exercise/ Flight training
	Wing fracture	3 - 6 weeks	Yes	Yes	Aviary exercise/ Flight training
	Gross feather damage	3 - 12 months	Yes	Yes	Aviary exercise/ Flight training
	Starvation	21 days	No	No	Aviary exercise/ Flight training
	Orphaned	N/A	N/A	N/A	Hacking/Tame hacking/Fostering
Small (insect eating) falcon					
	Head trauma	10 days	No	No	Aviary exercise
	Soft tissue damage	10 - 21 days	No	No	Aviary exercise
	Leg fracture	3 - 6 weeks	Yes	No	Aviary exercise
	Wing fracture	3 - 6 weeks	Yes	Yes	Aviary exercise
	Gross feather damage	3 - 12 months	Yes	Yes	Aviary exercise
	Starvation	21 days	No	No	Aviary exercise
	Orphaned	N/A	N/A	N/A	Hacking/Tame hacking/Fostering
True hawks (Goshawks and sparrow hawks)					
	Head trauma	10 days	No	No	Aviary exercise
	Soft tissue damage	10 - 21 days	Marginal	Yes	Aviary exercise
	Leg fracture	3 - 6 weeks	Yes	No	Aviary exercise/ Flight training
	Wing fracture	3 - 6 weeks	Yes	Yes	Aviary exercise/ Flight training
	Coracoid fracture	3 - 6 weeks	Yes	Yes	Aviary exercise/ Flight training
	Gross feather damage	3 - 12 months	Yes	Yes	Aviary exercise/ Flight training
	Starvation	21 days	No	No	Aviary exercise/ Flight training
	Orphaned	N/A	No	No	Hacking/Tame hacking/ Fostering
Buzzards/Harriers (Large and small)					
	Head trauma	10 days	No	No	Aviary exercise
	Soft tissue damage	10 - 21 days	No	No	Aviary exercise
	Leg fracture	3 - 6 weeks	Yes	No	Aviary exercise
	Wing fracture	3 - 6 weeks	Yes	Yes	Aviary exercise/ Flight training
	Gross feather damage	3 - 12 months	Yes	Yes	Aviary exercise/ Flight training
	Starvation	21 days	No	No	Aviary exercise
	Orphaned	N/A	N/A	N/A	Hacking/Tame hacking/Fostering

Species	Injury/other	Recovery time	Loss of fitness	Loss of flight ability	Rehab Method
Large eagles (Including fishing and snake eagles)					
	Head trauma	10 - 21 days	No	No	Aviary exercise
	Soft tissue damage	10 - 21 days	No	No	Aviary exercise
	Leg fracture	3 - 6 weeks	Yes	No	Aviary exercise/ Flight training*
	Wing fracture	3 - 6 weeks	Yes	Yes	Aviary exercise/ Flight training
	Gross feather damage	3 - 12 months	Yes	Yes	Aviary exercise/ Flight training
	Starvation	21 days	No	No	Aviary exercise
	Orphaned	N/A	N/A	N/A	Hacking/Tame hacking/Fostering
Small eagles (Hawk eagles and booted eagles)					
	Head trauma	10 days	No	No	Aviary exercise/ assessment/release
	Soft tissue damage	10 - 21 days	No	Yes	Aviary exercise and release
	Leg fracture	3 - 6 weeks	Yes	No	Aviary exercise/ Flight training
	Wing fracture	3 - 6 weeks	Yes	Yes	Aviary exercise/ Flight training
	Gross feather damage	3 - 12 months	Yes	Yes	Aviary exercise/ Flight training
	Starvation	21 days	No	No	Aviary exercise/ Flight training
	Orphaned	N/A	N/A	N/A	Hacking/Tame hacking/Fostering
Vultures (New and old world)					
	Head trauma	10 days	No	No	Aviary exercise
	Soft tissue damage	10 - 21 days	No	No	Aviary exercise
	Leg fracture	3 - 6 weeks	Yes	No	Aviary exercise
	Wing fracture	3 - 6 weeks	Yes	Yes	Aviary exercise
	Gross feather damage	3 - 12 months	Yes	Yes	Aviary exercise
	Starvation	21 days	No	No	Aviary exercise
	Orphaned	N/A	N/A	N/A	Hacking
Large and small owls (Horned to Scops owls)					
	Head trauma	10 days	No	No	Release post aviary assessment
	Soft tissue damage	10 - 21 days	No	Yes	Aviary exercise and release
	Leg fracture	3 - 6 weeks	Yes	No	
	Wing fracture	3 - 6 weeks	Yes	Yes	Aviary exercise and release
	Gross feather damage	3 - 12 months	Yes	Yes	Aviary exercise and release
	Starvation	21 days	Yes	Yes	Aviary assessment and release
	Orphaned	N/A	N/A	N/A	Hacking/Fostering

Table 2.6.2 Primary and secondary problems

Primary Injury	Secondary complications	Release viability	Exceptions
Head trauma	Eye damage/mandible damage	Poor	None
Soft tissue damage	Feather damage/Patagium contraction	Poor	Vultures/Harriers
Leg fracture	Bumble foot/Digit loss	Poor	Vultures
Wing fracture (Ulna/Radius/Humerus)	Wing extension deficit/ Feather damage	Poor	Vultures/Harriers
Coracoid fracture	Asymmetry	Poor	Vultures/Harriers
Gross feather damage	Follicle damage	Poor	None
Starvation	-	-	
Orphaned	Imprinting	Poor	None

2.7 AVIARY EXERCISE (FORCED EXERCISE)

Many rehabilitators are confined to basic rehabilitation methods, for example forced exercising of the bird within an aviary. This generally involves forcing the bird to fly up and down the length of the enclosure. Forced exercise, if conducted correctly, can achieve basic flight competence and lead to improved levels of fitness. For some species that have simple foraging strategies, this type of exercise may be adequate for rehabilitation.

Forced exercising must be conducted in a suitable enclosure. The larger the aviary the better, as it will be more versatile. Both large and small raptors do well in spacious aviaries. A large raptor should never be placed in a small aviary. The use of small enclosures, such as secondary care enclosures, for this purpose is not recommended, particularly for large raptors weighing over 500 grams. The length of these pens does not allow a raptor to gain enough speed to glide and thus land safe-ly. Most of the birds forced to exercise in these enclosures run the risk of damaging feet and feathers.

From the rehabilitator's point of view, the enclosure must be large enough to be able to accurately assess the bird's fitness and flight ability. Only after making an initial assessment can an effective exercise program be developed. A well-formulated program should have targets set throughout that will assist the raptor in gradually improving its flight ability and stamina. The final goal is to have a bird that is flight competent and can maintain its fitness levels. It will then be prepared for release into the wild.

Fitness is maintained by regular exercise, and by a regular and constant food intake that is above what is required for basic body main-tenance. In simple terms, if a raptor expends a certain number of calories in capturing prey, then it needs to replace those calories. If it constantly runs at a deficit, then it cannot maintain its lifestyle and cannot build and maintain fitness. Raptors that have been forced to rest due to injury invariably become unfit, despite having a constant food intake. Such loss of fitness is caused by lack of activity and is no different to that experienced by inactive human beings, or animals in captivity which are not exercised regularly.

2.7.1 General recommendations

A. For small raptors
Phase one: Preliminary (forced) flight exercise (introduction to the flight aviary)
• Aviary size: 80 ft. (25 m) length
• Number of flights per day: 5
• Total distance flown: 400 ft. (125 m) per day
• Duration: 10 days

Phase two: Secondary flight exercise
• Aviary size: 80 ft. (25 m) length
• Number of flights per day: 10
• Total distance flown: 800 ft. (250 m) per day
• Duration: 10 days

Phase three: Tertiary flight exercise
• Aviary size: 80 ft. (25 m) length
• Number of flights per day: 20
• Total distance flown: 1600 ft. (500 m) per day
• Duration: 10 days

B. For large raptors
Phase one: Preliminary (forced) flight exercise (introduction to the flight aviary)
• Aviary size: 165 ft. (50 m) length
• Number of flights per day: 5
• Total distance flown: 825 ft. (250 m) per day
• Duration: 10 days

Phase two: Secondary flight exercise
• Aviary size: 165 ft. (50 m) length
• Number of flights per day: 10
• Total distance flown: 1650 ft. (500 m) per day
• Duration: 10 days

Phase three: Tertiary flight exercise
• Aviary size: 165 ft. (50 m) length
• Number of flights per day: 30
• Total distance flown: 4950 ft. (1500 m) per day
• Duration: 10 days

If the raptor can complete the set number of flights in phase three with ease, then release can take place immediately. However, in the majority of cases, a newly recovered raptor will be unable to complete even the lowest number of flights without obvious signs of exhaustion.

Each bird's progress should be carefully monitored and properly recorded. A bird should not be forced to fly if it cannot manage the lowest number of repetitions (phase one), as shown in Table 2.7.2. It should be kept in mind that on very hot days the raptor will not be able to complete the set number of forced flights; its inability to do so under such circumstances should not always be regarded as an indication of a flight impairment.

The bird's fitness will improve with repeated exercise. The best indications of progress are the relative ease with which it manages the exercises and the length of time it takes to recover from the exertion. Recovery after exercise can be determined by visible indicators, such as the raptor's posture, the position of its wings, and whether or not it is gaping. During hot weather all raptors will try to cool down by gular fluttering (gaping).

An indication of the progress raptors should make when put through the same flight exercises with an increase in the number of flights per day (phase two) is shown in table 2.7.3. Careful monitoring of birds during this phase of training will give some indication as to whether or not they can be moved directly to the next stage (phase three), shown in table 2.7.4.

It must be pointed out that in all these stages factors such as flight symmetry, buoyancy, and landing ability should be carefully noted.

The fact that the bird is confined by the boundaries of the aviary should be taken into account, as it may be difficult to establish the raptor's overall maneuverability.

To sum up, let me say that the forced exercising of a bird in an aviary is a good option for some species under certain circumstances. It is suitable for searchers that have a simple foraging strategy and do not need to be actively trained (conditioned) and flown. It can also be used with attackers that have had a minor injury that can be addressed using an aviary. In all cases the aviary should be the correct size and constructed with suitable, safe materials. Forced exercise is risky, if not danger-ous, if the aviary is constructed from wire mesh. Collision with the mesh is inevitable, and often disastrous. In an ideal world, this type of flight would take place in a long sealed corridor with perches at both ends.

Many rehabilitators are confined to using an aviary for a variety of species and circum-stances, either because of financial con-straints, lack of experience with other methods, or general philosophical beliefs. In the event a rehabilitator is presented with a seriously injured attacker requiring more sophisticated rehabilitation, then flight train-ing is a better option.

C. Species specific recommendations

Table 2.7.2 Phase one aviary exercise routines

Species*	Flights expected	Flights completed	Recovery time	Repeat
Peregrine**	5	2	20 minutes	No
Peregrine**	5	4	15 minutes	No
Peregrine **	5	5	15 minutes	No
Goshawk	5	5	17 minutes	No
Large Eagle	5	2	20 minutes	No
Kestrel	5	3	10 minutes	No
Small falcon	5	5	7 minutes	No
Small falcon	5	2	12 minutes	No

*   Raptors recovered from fractured Ulna.
     Recovery time — when respiration returned to normal (Lactic acid levels are also a good indicator).
** Same bird within the 10 day period

Table 2.7.3 Phase two exercise routines

Species	Flights expected	Flights completed	Recovery time	Repeat
Peregrine	10	10	10 minutes	No
Peregrine	10	10	10 minutes	No
Peregrine	10	10	10 minutes	No
Goshawk	10	9	12 minutes	No
Eagle	10	8	14 minutes	Yes
Kestrel	10	10	6 minutes	No
Small falcon	10	10	5 minutes	No

Table 2.7.4 Phase three exercise regimes for specific species.

Species	Flights expected	Flights completed	Recovery time	Repeat.
Peregrine	20	20	10 minutes	No
Peregrine	20	20	10 minutes	No
Peregrine	20	20	10 minutes	No
Brown goshawk	20	27	12 minutes	No
Wedge-tailed eagle	20	19	10 minutes	No
Australian kestrel	20	20	-*	No
Little falcon	20	20	-*	No
Little falcon	20	20	-*	No

* No recovery time noted.
** No accurate temperatures taken.

2.7.5 Flight training (encouraged exercise)

Flight training (see chapter 6, Training methods) is perhaps an inappropriate term to use for encouraged flight exercise. The connotations of the word training, for some rehabilitators, are often shocking, for they include weight reductions, possible imprinting, and obvious taming, which could be detrimental to the ultimate survival of the raptor involved. It is, however, possible to use certain minimum conditioning processes to encourage rather than force flight.

Before looking at the training process, two types of exercise which are effective in improving overall fitness and basic flight competence are worth discussing; these are vertical flight and corridor flying. Once again, the rehabilitator should consider the bird in question and decide whether it needs extensive flight training. A raptor can take time to condition; behaviors have to be set and food consumption controlled. It may be better in some cases to use a forced exercise regime, particularly when simple flight assessment is the only requirement.

A. Vertical flight

Many falconers and rehabilitators use vertical flight as an exercise, but it is important to remember these points:

1. Raptors (particularly goshawks) can jump quite high, so the vertical flight should be a flight as opposed to a mere jump with a quick wing-flap.
2. The angle at which the bird flies to a perch or glove should not be too steep (30 degrees is good).
3. Approximately 10 ft. (3 m) from a perch to the gloved hand or to a perch with food, is a good height for this exercise.
4. The exercises should gradually be build up from a small number of flights, say ten in one session, to a higher number as the bird improves in general physical condition.

A variation of vertical flight is gradient flight. This is perhaps self-explanatory, as the raptor is encouraged to fly at a 45 degree angle to a point where the food is located. The flight down is also good exercise, as the bird really has to back beat to slow down and land. This works well for large eagles.

B. Corridor flying

Many large rehabilitation centers use this type of exercise for eagles and buzzards. The flight distance is generally about 80–160 ft. (25–50 m). The exercise takes place within an enclosed corridor with perches at both ends. The raptor is encouraged to fly from end to end for a small food reward. This can also be a forced exercise regime and may be appropriate if large numbers of birds are being dealt with, or when the injury is minor and the expected recovery time is short.

C. Creance flying

Evaluating flight can be achieved in an open field by using a creance or safety line. Jesses or anklets and a swivel are attached to the bird's tarsi. A length of nylon cord, 5 mm in diameter, at least 650 ft. (200 m) long is then tied onto the swivel or directly to the jesses. The free end of the line is tied to a piece of wood, which will act as a drag and should weigh no less than 50% of the bird's total weight. Two people are needed for this operation. One person holds the line near the drag while the other releases the bird into the wind.

It is vital that the person holding the line runs as the bird flies and gently drags it down when required. The line should never be tied to a solid object.

Evaluation of the raptor's flight ability can take place on the spot, or by using a video camera. This process can be repeated a number of times, however, this method should be avoided on very hot days. It is important to undertake this process only in an open area entirely clear of trees, fences, and power lines. Sports fields are perfect for this exercise.

While both vertical flight and corridor flying can be useful in assessing a bird's basic flight competence, these exercises offer no indication of its foraging ability. In the rehabilitation context, flight competence and fitness is useless unless it exists in conjunction with foraging competence. In order to catch prey, a raptor must be physically and mentally fit. A raptor that is fit and bt has no foraging experience will be at a serious disadvantage when it is forced to compete on equal terms with raptors that have all three survival pre-requisites.

2.8 DEALING WITH ORPHANED RAPTORS

Raptors are orphaned for a variety of reasons: owls that have left the nest-hollow or wandered away from the nest are often found by well-meaning passers-by and passed on to rehabilitators; nest collapse or the loss of parents is another cause for raptor chicks becoming orphaned.

The objective of artificially rearing young orphaned raptors is to see them through the development stage and then through to eventual release and final dispersal. Rearing raptors for demonstration purposes does not differ, although in this case it is often desirable to socially imprint the individuals. Creche rearing, or rearing groups of chicks together, whether siblings or otherwise, is preferable to rearing individuals in isolation. Group rearing can also be done in an aviary when broods of orphans are being dealt with. It is a good idea to house unreleasable adult and juvenile birds next door to the chicks, as this allows some social development to take place.

Very few wildlife rehabilitators have to deal with raptors that are less than ten days old.

Illustration: Elizabeth Darby

From this age onward, most young raptors can be encouraged to self-feed from a bowl of chopped meat. It is unfortunate that many hand-reared raptors become behaviorally isolated and unreleasable. Such imprinting can be avoided if care is taken, but realistically, it is virtually impossible to hand rear raptors less than ten days old in total isolation from others with a reasonable expectation of normal development unless the chick is prevented from seeing humans and only fed by a puppet.

Raptors develop in stages. From hatching to the appearance of the first down the young bird needs to be brooded by the female almost constantly to keep warm. As size increases, the second down appears and helps in self-insulation. Later in this stage the young are often too big to be brooded by the female. The second down coincides with the emergence of primary and tail feathers, referred to as "pins."

Fledging is not the first true flight, as many raptor species leave the nest well before they can fly. They simply outgrow the nest and move off into surrounding branches or rocks, depending on the type of nest site. Many species are still fully dependent on their parents well after their first flight, and only attain independence as their flight and foraging skills develop. The period from fledging to full independence can take as little as three weeks in some small species to as much as six months in the large species. Table 2.8.1 shows the development of different species of raptor chicks.

Table 2.8.1. Raptor chick development, fledging to independence.

Species	First down	Second down	First flight	Independence*	Reference
Peregrine falcon	4 days	14 days	40 days	75–90 days	1, 2
Hobby	4 days	14 days	35 days	70–80 days	1, 2
Kestrel	4 days	9 days	30 days	21 days	1, 2
Goshawk	3–4 days	12 days	26–31 days	21–35 days	1, 2
Bald eagle	0–10 days	10+ days	80–90 days	180 days	3
True eagle	10 days	21 days	70 days	180 days	1, 2
Buzzard	10 days	21 days	50–60 days	150 days	1, 2

* Days to independence after first flight.

References.
1. Handbook of Australian, New Zealand and Antarctic Birds, Vol.2.
2. Birds of prey of Southern Africa, Peter Steyn.
3. David Hancock, personal correspondence.

It is always a good idea to identify what species you are dealing with and determine the chick's age. There are various methods in practice that will allow you to ascertain the bird's age if the wing pins (feathers) are showing. These formulas were derived by measuring the wing chords (the measurement from the carpal joint to the tip of the longest primary feather) of birds of known age at various stages in their development. The measurements for certain species are shown in table 2.8.2. While this might seem totally irrelevant in terms of hand raising, it should be of great assistance when it comes to the hacking process (see this chapter). Many orphaned raptors are picked up during the second part of their development, when the primary feathers are half-developed.

Where specific comparative data is not available the raptor rehabilitator should keep such growth records and publish them for future comparisons.

Table 2.8.2 Ascertaining age in days. Specific examples.

Species	Wing chord/ age in days	Wing chord/ age in days	Wing chord/ age in days	References
Brown goshawk	11.4 cm / 17 days	17.5 cm / 25 days	25.5 cm / 37 days	1, 2, 3
Sparrowhawk	11.4 cm / 18 days	17.5 cm / 27 days	25.5 cm / 40 days	1, 2, 3
Peregrine	13.0 cm / 20 days	16.0 cm / 24 days	25.0 cm / 37 days	1, 2, 3
Australian hobby	13.0 cm / 22 days	16.0 cm / 27 days	25.0 cm / 41 days	1, 2, 3
Brown falcon	13.0 cm / 20 days	16.0 cm / 24 days	25.0 cm / 37 days	1, 2, 3
Booted eagle	13.0 cm / 24 days	16.0 cm / 29 days	25.0 cm / 43 days	1, 2, 3
Whistling kite	13.0 cm / 26 days	16.0 cm / 30 days	25.0 cm / 44 days	1, 2, 3

References   1. *Handbook of Australian, New Zealand & Antarctic Birds.*
2. Olsen, P.D. & J. Olsen. 1981. *Raptor Research* 15: 53–57.
3. Healesville Sanctuary Raptor Rehabilitation Program. *Unpublished Data.*

Raptors grow quickly. In most cases, just before they fledge they have attained, or exceeded, adult weight. During the development period, food quality is crucial and periods between feeds should be short. In the wild, young peregrine falcons up to a week old are fed, on average, once every hour. The time between feeds increases as the chicks grow. Begging actions from the chicks will evoke a feeding response from the parent; if the chick doesn't beg, the parent will not feed it. When the young are very small, the female may vocalize and try to solicit a begging response. Young falcons will sit up and beg quite loudly; on the other hand, young hawks need to be stimulated to feed and are more likely to lunge at the food. Feeding with sharp forceps is dangerous, particularly if the young hawk is a lunger. Blunting the ends of the forceps or using blunt wooden tongs will reduce the risk of eye damage to young chicks.

2.8.3 So what is needed to rear a young raptor?

1. A brooder box (a box that is thermostatically controlled).
2. A set of accurate scales (electronic with a graduation of one gram or less).
3. Blunt-ended forceps.
4. A supply of fresh food.
5. Feeder seclusion, or the use of puppets to reduce imprinting on humans.

The brooder box should be kept at a temperature of 30C (86F) for the first 10 days. This temperature can be gradually reduced as the chick starts to self-regulate its body temperature. In the wild, the second down insulates the chicks when the female cannot brood them. The chicks themselves are excellent indicators of whether or not they are too hot or too cold; if they are too warm, they will sprawl, and if too cold, they will huddle.

Each chick should be weighed before and after each feed, as this will give you an indication of 1) the weight increment, and 2) the amount of food eaten per meal.

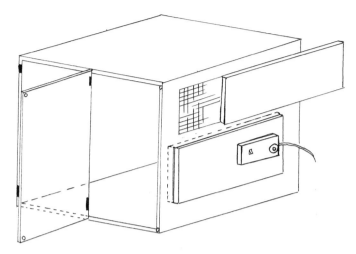

Figure 2.8.3 Brooder box.

2.9 PREPARING THE FOOD

Food preparation is important. Do not re-use food that has not been eaten and do not re-freeze uneaten food. Take out enough for one meal and make sure it is at room temperature before feeding. Food should be prepared as follows:

2.9.1 Chicks aged 1–10 days

A. Rat and mouse preparation.
1. Skin the rodent and remove the head, feet, tail and intestines.
2. Mince the body using a mincing machine or a mallet; make sure it is finely crushed.
3. Prepare enough food for the day.

B. Feeding regime: feed every two hours. This is a rough guide; only feed if the gut or crop is partially or totally empty.

2.9.2 Chicks aged 10–15 days

A. Rat and mouse preparation.
1. Skin the rodent, remove the head, tail and intestines.
2. Chop up the animal, not too finely.
3. Make sure the portions are not too big.

B. Feeding regime: feed every four hours. Again, this is a rough guide; only offer feed when the gut or crop is empty or partially so.

At this age the chicks should be able to feed from a bowl. Falcon chicks are easily taught to self-feed. Not only does this save time and allow them some independence, but prevents the development of any strong association between humans and food.

2.9.3 Chicks aged 15–25 days and eagle chicks to fledging

A. Whole food can be provided.
1. Skinned and gutted rodents.
2. Plucked quail, opened to expose the meat.

B. Feeding regime: feed ad-lib; preferably leave food for the whole day and replace it when necessary.

At this stage, make sure that each chick is getting its fair share of food. Offer the last feed at sunset.

2.10 BEHAVIORAL DEVELOPMENT

The behavior of a raptor is partially innate (the black-breasted buzzard knows how to break eggs with a rock), partially imprinted, and partially learned.

Instinctive behavior includes search methods and reproductive behavior, and to some extent, the fear of certain species. As examples, falcons generally react adversely to true hawks, such as goshawks, and many raptors will react to owls.

Imprinted behavior includes identification of parents and siblings, and fear responses; young birds are also imprinted on the type of nesting site used by the species. Imprint behaviors are learned almost automatically when the developing chick is subjected to specific stimuli at specific times in its development.

Learned behavior is more complex. What sounds mean food and when to expect food through visual cues are all learned. Screaming for food is an example. In the wild state, young raptors learn how to recognize potential danger and intruders at the nest: other species of raptor, and human beings. They learn how to respond to social cues and interact with siblings. The correct combination of all these behaviors will produce the ideal bird for release; the incorrect combination will not.

Behavioral traits learned during rearing are outlined in Table 2.10.1.

Table 2.10.1. Behavioral traits learned during rearing.

Wild parent-reared	Partially human-reared	Totally human-reared	References
Has fear response.	Partial fear response.	No fear response of humans.	1, 2
Recognizes own kind.	Responds to both human and own species.	Has abnormal fear response of own kind.	1, 2
Begs from own species.	Will beg from humans and own species *	No normal begging response to own species. Solicits food from humans.*	1, 2
Not aggressive toward humans	Shows some food-associated aggression	Treats humans as siblings/potential threat to food, is defensive over food.	1, 2
Courts own species	Courts both	Courts humans only	1, 2

*Screaming for food is often associated with imprinted behavior, but prior to becoming independent, a young raptor will scream for food regardless of its rearing.

References: 1. Nick Fox, *Understanding the Bird of Prey*, 1995.
                    2. Personal observations.

2.10.2 Crucial periods

Young raptors first imprint onto their parents and then their siblings. They develop a fear response to things that are not a part of their daily lives, for example intruders at the nest. The reaction of their parents to intruders or to objects that cause alarm will in turn reinforce their fear response. They learn how to socialize and therefore how to select and recognize future potential sexual partners. Finally, when they are free flying, they can develop an image of where they were born and thus recognize future nesting sites.

The crucial periods of the raptor's behavioral development are as follows:

1. Day 1–20   Parental imprinting.
2. Day 10–25   Sibling recognition or imprinting.

3. Day 10–25 Development of fear responses.
4. Day 20–45 Future sexual partner recognition.
5. Day 35–independence:
   Nest site recognition.

In summing up this section on rearing young raptors, the development period is just as important as food and food consumption.

The following should be remembered:

1. Pay attention to the age of the raptor; confirm the species.
2. Adhere to correct feeding regimes.
3. Provide the correct diet.
4. Keep accurate records.
5. Seek expert veterinary attention if problems arise.
6. Keep the chicks isolated as much as possible from seeing humans to reduce imprinting.

2.11 RE-INTRODUCING ORPHANED RAPTORS

2.11.1 Traditional hacking.

Broods of young raptors can be traditionally hacked in a hack box. The purpose of this method is to allow a natural fledging process to take place. Groups of chicks will generally stick together until dispersal, and in the process they can learn the appropriate search and attack behaviors and all the social graces required for future pairings and socializing. Single orphans which are hacked are at a serious disadvantage in terms of social development; by not having a sibling group to interact with, they are likely to wander off well before they are ready. As a group, the orphans will keep in contact with each other, either vocally or visually. Anyone who has ever watched wild eagles or falcons and their fledged young will understand the importance of this cohesiveness.

It is important to place the orphans in the hack box at the right time in their physical development (see Section 2.7). It is vital that the young birds are self-feeding from a bowl well before they are placed in the hack box; once they are inside, food should be placed in the box twice per day. All the precautions to prevent any food/human associations from developing must be taken.

For small raptors, the dimensions of the hack box should be 3 ft. x 3 ft. x 3 ft. (1 m x 1 m x 1 m). The front should be slatted with vertical slats and open downward, in order to serve as a ledge when open. The box must be placed high enough off the ground to reduce the risk of mammalian predators gaining

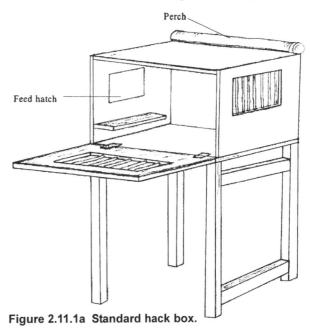

Figure 2.11.1a Standard hack box.

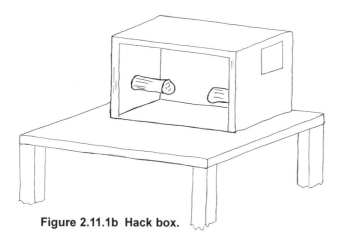

Figure 2.11.1b Hack box.

access once the door has been finally opened. The position and location must be chosen carefully for food availability and safety; it is madness to place a brood of orphaned peregrines in a hack box that is near a highway, power lines, or private pigeon lofts. Final dispersal of the birds will take place at varying times. Some species will become independent quite quickly, while others can take three months before they are totally self-sufficient.

For large raptors, the dimensions should be increased proportionally; a hack box measuring 6 ft. x 6 ft. x 6 ft. (2 m x 2 m x 2 m) should suffice.

A. Hacking from start to finish.
1. Ten day old orphaned kestrel chicks are checked for injuries; all seem fine.
2. Feeding regime is established.
3. Weight increment is steady.
4. Feathers start to appear and the orphans become more mobile.
5. The young birds are placed in the hack box and taken to the release site.
6. Enough food for all the birds is left.
7. A check is made the following morning; any food that has not been eaten is removed and new food is left.
8. Feeding and checks carry on until the chicks are close to twenty-five days old.
9. Food left in the box via a hatch and the door is opened as quietly as possible.

10. The first bird leaves the box for a quick exploratory flight; observations are kept up.
11. Two weeks have passed since the box was first opened. The chicks spend more and more time away from the box.
12. All the chicks have dispersed five weeks later.

B. What could go wrong with this process?
- If the box is not in a secure position, predators could easily gain access and kill the newly fledged raptors. Potential predators include avian, reptilian, and mammalian.
- Disturbance just after the box has been opened could result in premature fledging, with the young raptors dispersing in panic.
- If the box is placed in an area where there are other species of raptors breeding, then there is a risk of the young birds being predated upon.

To understand what traditional hacking is intended to achieve, one needs to be familiar with the whole process of fledging, and the subsequent achievement of independence and survival. Traditional hacking can only offer the chance of a natural fledge. Remember that the young birds will be dependent on supplementary food in the hack box for varying lengths of time. Large eagles and large falcons take a long time to gain independence, so the rehabilitator must be patient in waiting for their final dispersal. With traditional hacking there is no control over where the fledged raptors go, and unless they are being radio tracked with transmitters, their ultimate fate will be unknown. Traditional hacking is not recommended for single orphans; rather, such birds should be tame hacked, unless the situation arises where the rehabilitator has no other alternative.

2.11.2 Tame hacking

Tame hacking can be used to reintroduce single orphans to the wild, particularly if there are no other viable options for release, although, ideally, single orphans should be placed with other orphans of the same age and then traditionally hacked or fostered out to wild pairs that have offspring. The single orphan will need to be reared carefully to avoid imprinting to humans. This is difficult unless one has access to birds that are unreleasable, to which the young bird can be exposed in adjacent pens (see Section 2.8).

Tame hacking is a modified version of the traditional wild hack. It allows a great deal more control over the orphan in terms of when and where it is allowed to exercise. In choosing tame hack sites, one should follow the same rules used in selecting traditional hack sites. Avoid areas where human habitation is high or where there are highways close by. Eagles should not be hacked where there is a likelihood of them encountering livestock. It is also worth while to inform all the local residents that a raptor is being rehabilitated or reintroduced in the area. I recommend using transmitters on all tame hacked raptors, as it is then possible to follow their progress closely when they are not visible or when they have left the hack site.

Only one species at a time may be tame hacked in the same area; to tame hack three or four different species of birds, a separate site must be found for each. The whole process will be time consuming for one person. When a rehabilitator is confronted with this situation and has a number of orphans of varying species, he should consider each individually. Species with a simple search and attack strategy should be traditionally hacked, and those that have a more complex hunting method should be tame hacked. Single red-tailed hawk or common buzzard orphans can be traditionally hacked. This may not be ideal, but it is better than simply throwing them out. Large falcons need to be tame hacked. Eagles also benefit from tame hacking, although this is incredibly time consuming. Golden eagles need to be hacked well away from habitation.

The raptor should be introduced to the tame hacking release site well before it can fly; it can be fed at the site from a low block on the ground. An artificial nest can be placed in a tree crotch; an old tire covered with astroturf is ideal for this purpose. Late afternoon is the best time to start the orientation. Allow about

Figure 2.11.2a
Bald eagle chick reared for tame hacking being fed using a puppet to avoid imprinting to humans.
Photo: Sutton Research Center

Figure 2.11.2b Nine-week-old bald eagle chick.
Photo: David Hancock

sixty minutes for the initial sessions. First, place the orphan on the nest and let it look around. It can be fed either on a lure or by just leaving food on the nest. If introduced early, a lure is handy for falcons and eagles. A whistle will also help, as the bird can then be called to the rehaber later on in its training.

The time that the bird is allowed to spend at the release site should increase as flight potential increases. Start with a sixty minute session, just before sunset, and gradually increase to eighty minutes, and so on, by starting earlier in the day, until finally the bird is out all day. This process can take three to five weeks, and the rehabilitator can either spend the whole day at the site or simply leave and return later to check on or retrieve the bird. Transmitters are especially handy at this time. Once the raptor is flying well and is able to find a secure roosting area, it can be left out overnight. The rehabilitator should remember, however, to first check for the threat of any

large owls in the vicinity.

The whole point of a tame hack is to allow some orientation to the release site and to give the rehabilitator a chance to monitor the bird's progress and to continue to supply food well after fledging, if required. A well-fed raptor at tame hack will still try to hunt and seek independence. I have had falcons at tame hack for nine weeks, after which they were not only aloof, but efficiently feeding themselves. One falcon still remains in the same area after four years and is now breeding there with another, more recently tame hacked bird.

A tame hacked bird does not need to be tethered or fitted with permanent jesses, but it will need to be fitted with a leg-mounted transmitter until the tail has fully emerged. Once the raptor is being left out overnight, it will become more aloof. If a tail-mounted transmitter has to be attached to replace the leg-mounted unit, the bird will need to be trapped and fitted with the new transmitter, and the leg-mounted one removed. As time progresses, the raptor will become less punctual; at times, it will not be at the site when the rehabilitator arrives. When this happens, it is useful to try to locate the bird; if this is not possible, one can simply wait until the next day and try again.

Dispersal normally takes place soon after independence has been attained, and this comes with self-sufficiency in terms of finding and catching food. With species that are migratory or nomadic, there is an urge to disperse as the season progresses from summer into autumn. For this reason, some raptors that have been injured before they reach full independence will actually be racing against time, or rather the rehabilitator will be, for the raptor will leave the hack site whether you are confident of its ability to survive or not.

Tame hacking can also be applied to individuals that have been injured after their first full flight, but before becoming fully independent, or to those that have had their foraging competence reduced by injury. This works well with juveniles, but not so efficiently with adults that have been breeding or were breeding prior to injury. These adults will invariably disperse to their breeding territories as soon as they are liberated. Therefore, one should always make sure that an adult bird is competent before its total release.

Dealing with wild-fledged raptors, as opposed to captive-fledged, in the tame hack capacity will require the use of jesses, either removable clip-ons or anklets that are more permanent. This method of tame hack requires more contact between the bird and the rehabilitator. During exercise periods in the release area it is important to watch how the bird copes. The objective is to assess its flight competence and allow this to improve. Foraging ability and ultimate proficiency will come with time and effort. The bird needs to develop a full repertoire of search and attack strategies. At times it may be appropriate to assist the bird, always remembering that the bird at tame hack is not a falconry bird and will ultimately be released, and must therefore develop strategies without human intervention. If the raptor can succeed repeatedly in difficult circumstances, this will augur well for its future in the wild.

It is a good idea to compare the search and attack strategies used by the bird one is dealing with to those that have been recorded for that particular species in the wild. The typical waiting-on flight for a peregrine, a gyrfalcon, or saker falcon might be desirable for the falconer who wants to witness a spectacular stoop, but the falcon at hack may use less classical strategies which prove to be efficient in its circumstances. The bird must be allowed to experiment and learn. This will be to its ultimate advantage, and is also reassuring to the rehabilitator who observes the process.

Goshawks are slightly different. Their attack strategies are comparatively straightforward but prey selection is more complex. A direct attack from a perch is their standard approach when pursuing prey. One of the best methods for developing hunting skills in a goshawk is to let it follow you as you walk. In Africa, the chanting-goshawks often follow livestock or their herders, and in Australia, brown goshawks sometimes follow horseback riders in the hope of catching some prey animal that has been disturbed from cover.

Eagles are more problematic, and yet in some ways they are easier to tame hack than most other species. Tawny eagles, wedge-tailed eagles, steppe eagles, and golden eagles occasionally feed upon carrion, which can be easily found in some areas, although at certain times of the year carrion will be scarce. Thus there is still a need for the eagle to develop search and attack skills. Many eagle species have a long dependency period and will therefore require an extended tame hack–they need time to learn.

Figure 2.11.2c
Temporary anklets clipped on with a press stud.

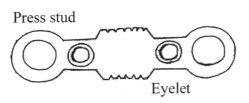

Press stud

Eyelet

Any species of bird can be tame hacked and many people carry out the process without really knowing or understanding what they are doing. The tame hack that involves a relative hands-off approach, as with pre-fledged raptors, will be time consuming; a more direct hands-on tame hack will be even more so. The rehabilitator must understand the whole process and think very carefully about what he is doing. If he is confined by time constraints, lack of release sites or legal restraints, then the bird should be passed on to a person who can devote both the time and energy required.

2.12 THE STARVING RAPTOR

The raptor rehabilitator is frequently confronted by the starving raptor; this could represent any species ranging from hawks and eagles to owls and falcons. The primary concern in these situations is that the raptor's general condition be improved, which can be achieved by care and feeding. Experience is a decided asset when dealing with raptors that are significantly malnourished, and it is particularly important here to have an idea of the correct weight for its sex, age, and species.

Raptors that are presented to the rehabilitator with no visible injuries, but which are severely emaciated, have had a problem either through parasite burdens or a simple inability to compete with others of the same species for a scarce food resource. A thorough examination should narrow down the cause of the starvation. A broad spectrum treatment for parasites should be administered to reduce that burden.

Winter is the time when the majority of raptors are found starving. More often than not they are juveniles facing the test of hunting on their own under difficult circumstances. Even though the bird may have been treated for parasite burdens, its inability to forage competently still remains. Adult birds, which have a wide repertoire of search and attack strategies, cope much better when their prey base is reduced; juveniles do not cope as well and often face starvation—in short, nature's adjustment of predators to fit the reduced food supply. In reality, there is a high juvenile mortality rate caused by starvation. A young goshawk or peregrine that is finding it difficult to meet its daily energy requirements will start to weaken, and the more hunting attempts it makes, the more energy it expends, until it no longer has the strength to fly. This becomes a vicious circle, inevitably ending in death if the bird is not subjected to rehabilitation.

Low prey populations pose something of a dilemma to the rehabilitator who is dealing with a starving raptor. Several options are available. The first is to feed the bird until it has attained maximum weight once again and then release it in an area where the prey base is adequate. The second option is to actively train and fly the bird, thus giving it some additional foraging experience. The third alternative is to hold it over until spring, when weather and food conditions improve, and then release it. The rehabilitator who has no experience in flight training techniques is limited to the first option, but the rehabilitator who can properly flight train a bird may choose either the second or third, depending upon the amount of time he can devote to the bird. Understanding these options is an important factor in the final decision, as it is often not practical for a rehabilitator to flight train every bird he receives.

Chapter Three
Releasing Rehabilitated Raptors

3.1 Choosing Release Sites

When choosing a release site, the two primary considerations, from the bird's perspective, are safety from immediate danger and a stable and existing food supply suitable for, and accessible to, the species being released. The release site should be free of potential hazards, including vehicle traffic, power lines, fences, and vulnerable livestock such as lambs, poultry, etc. Once a prospective area has been deemed safe, then equal emphasis must be placed on the availability of prey suitable for the individual bird being released, otherwise the effort is pointless, as the released bird will have no incentive to remain near the release site. For example, a kestrel should be released in a habitat specifically chosen because it harbors numerous small mammals and invertebrates. Similarly, the area selected for releasing a peregrine must support an abundance of small birds. When releasing a bald eagle, the presence of a suitable supply of carrion, such as the carcasses of spawning salmon, can be an important factor in effectively introducing the bird back to the wild. A readily available food supply appropriate to the species will encourage raptors to stay in the release area for at least a few days, and at times, juveniles will remain for a couple of weeks or even months if they are being tame or wild hacked. In most cases, however, a raptor that is not being tame or traditionally hacked will not stay at the release site, but will move on quite quickly.

It is vital to remember that prey must not only be present, but must also be accessible to the species being released. One of the biggest mistakes a rehabilitator can make is to assume that because a release area has a multitude of prey species, it will automatically be suitable for a raptor's release. Whether or not the raptor will be able to forage effectively must be taken into account. This can be influenced by a number of factors, including the type of terrain and grass length. Kestrels, for instance, are unable to access insects in heavy grass over thirty centimeters in length. On the other hand, black-shouldered kites, brown falcons, and harriers can still-hunt in such habitat very effectively. As further examples, harriers cannot gain access to rodents in scrub country, and goshawks actually require woodlands or stands of trees from which to search and launch attacks.

3.1.1 Assessing release sites

The relative availability of food can be ascertained by careful observation. Taking a walk over an open paddock to look for invertebrates and small mammals will give an indication of food availability; however, one must remember to check these areas at a time of day when these prey items are active and when the predator is accustomed to hunting.

3.1.2 Prey density

A release site with a high density of prey is an important consideration, especially when releasing juveniles. A juvenile needs a prey base up to 4 times greater than that required by an adult, in order to find the more easily caught prey. To clarify this, an adult hawk might find a vulnerable prey from a flock of 25 birds, while a juvenile might need a flock of 100 birds from which to choose the vulnerable individual. This fact has greater relevance for the more dynamic or attacking species of raptor, including the peregrine, merlin, gyrfalcon, and goshawk. Searchers are often nomadic, and will move from area to area, usually staying in one location only as long as the habitat can support a large prey base. The black-shouldered kite is a typical example of this; these kites may appear in large numbers in any given year if the food supply, e.g., rodents, is readily available.

To conclude, when assessing a release site the considerations are as follows: a) the site is safe, b) the site has suitable prey species for the raptor being released, c) there is sufficient prey density, d) prey is accessible. These basic rules apply to birds that are being released after a brief period of rest and recovery, or after being tame or wild hacked. Prey availability can only be assessed at the release site; once the raptor leaves the area, all one can do is hope that it will seek out areas with a similar prey density.

CHAPTER FOUR
MONITORING RELEASED BIRDS

4.1 POST RELEASE MONITORING

The rehabilitator will never know if the rehabilitation process has been successful unless he can follow the progress of released raptors. It is important to know the fate of at least some birds in order to justify the long and expensive efforts, and to refine rehabilitation techniques in the future. Radio telemetry is the only reliable way of ascertaining the survival of released animals. Radio tracking can assist in locating released raptors, and by discreet monitoring, their condition can be evaluated. The movement of birds after release can be plotted, and their eventual survival or death can be confirmed; only from this information can the rehabilitation methods be assessed.

4.2 USING TRANSMITTERS

All wildlife rehabilitators should have some basic knowledge of this useful equipment and how it functions. The type of transmitter may vary depending upon its range of use. For instance, falconry transmitters differ from research tracking units. Falconers prefer the advantage of a light transmitter that simply sends out a signal to locate a lost bird, while researchers require more detailed information. Transmitters for rehabilitation should offer more than just the ability to locate a bird after release. In many cases it is important to know if the bird is dead, alive, or just sleeping. The more functions a transmitter is capable of performing, the more expensive it will be, so it is wise to opt for the bare minimum if budgetary constraints exist. Another consideration is time spent in the field. Is it really worth while radio tracking a kestrel, spending the time and money on a common species?

In tracking released raptors, what does one want to know?

1. Where the bird goes.
2. How it forages.
3. Its hunting success.
4. Eventual survival.

All the above points have greater ramifications than just "knowing" what a bird does after release. We can assess the usefulness of various rehabilitation methods from the raptor's foraging success or failure, and adjust and improve our methods accordingly.

Locating a raptor, or monitoring its movements after release, can be comparatively simple using radio transmitters. The position of the bird should be checked three times daily, first thing in the morning, around midday, and at sunset. This is less time consuming than direct observation when assessing foraging competency, hunting success, or ultimate survival.

Transmitters come in various styles. Without going into the essential circuitry or the components that make them up, suffice it to say that they are designed to not be a physical encumbrance to the bird. It would defeat the purpose if the weight or the bulk of a transmitter restricted the bird's movement, hampered its foraging ability, or otherwise made life difficult for the wearer. The designs are constantly changing. Seven years ago the smallest satellite transmitter I could find weighed 100 grams; today, many units weigh as little as 25 grams.

4.3 MOUNTING TRANSMITTERS

Transmitter placement is just as important as the transmitter itself. Incorrectly mounted and inappropriate transmitters can cause problems for raptors. Under many circumstances they can even prove dangerous. Unlike mammals, it is not a viable option to use a collar on a raptor. However, three other types of mounts have been developed for use with raptors and other birds.

4.3.1 Leg mounts

Many falconers will not use leg-mounted transmitters for fear of entanglement, but in cases where a raptor is being tame hacked and its tail feathers have not yet fully emerged, a leg-mounted transmitter is vital. This can be replaced with a tail mounted unit once the tail feathers have totally emerged and hardened. Leg mounts can also be used on demonstration birds, where the risk of entanglement is greatly reduced. Leg-mounted transmitters are more useful if the aerial, or antenna, is not flexible or too long, i.e., over 21 centimeters in length.

4.3.2 Tail mounts

Tail-mounted transmitters are invariably shed when the raptor molts. If the antenna protrudes beyond the tail tip and is flexible, entanglement becomes a serious possibility, particularly when the raptor is flying over fences. Many falconers who use tail-mounted transmitters have experienced problems with the central tail feathers being ripped out after becoming caught on a fence. Most research transmitters do not have very flexible antennae, and this helps to reduce this risk.

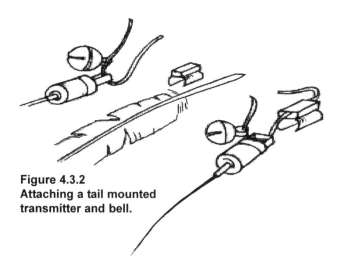

**Figure 4.3.2
Attaching a tail mounted
transmitter and bell.**

4.3.3 Harness/back-pack mounts

This type of mounting is designed to break off if the raptor becomes caught in vegetation or on a fence. In some cases, the raptor can carry a heavier load if it is placed on the back, but even then the total weight of the package should not exceed 5% of the raptor's total body weight.

Types of transmitters I have used success-fully with raptors of different species, sexes, and weights are listed in Table 4.3.4. Additional data on transmitters used on raptors in falconry and in a rehabilitation context are provided in Table 4.3.5. If one is unsure of what type of transmitter to use, or where to place it, he should always seek the advice of someone with more extensive experience. The consequences of making assumptions could be disastrous.

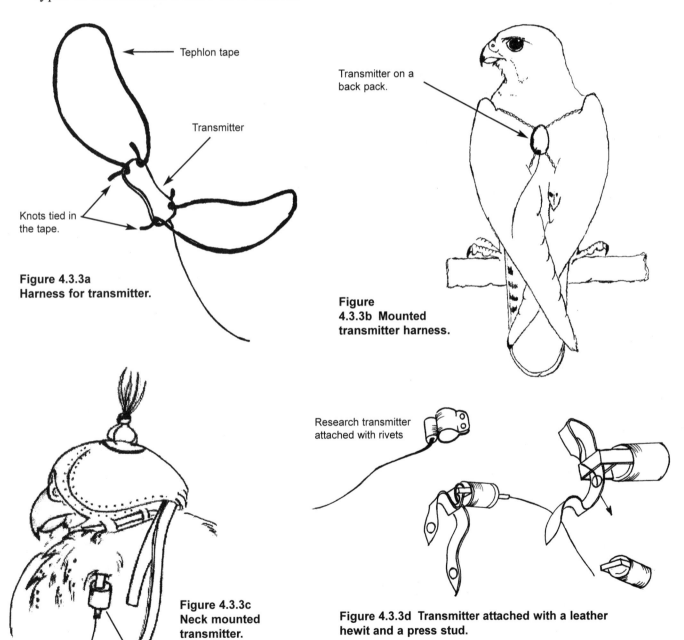

Tephlon tape

Transmitter

Knots tied in the tape.

**Figure 4.3.3a
Harness for transmitter.**

Transmitter on a back pack.

Figure 4.3.3b Mounted transmitter harness.

Figure 4.3.3c Neck mounted transmitter.

Research transmitter attached with rivets

Figure 4.3.3d Transmitter attached with a leather hewit and a press stud.

Table 4.3.4 Transmitters used on rehabilitated raptors

Species	Sex	Weight	Transmitter weight	Mounting	Number
Peregrine	Female	890 grams	9 grams	Tail	5
Peregrine	Male	560 grams	7 grams	Leg	1
Australian hobby	Female	310 grams	7 grams	Tail	3
Australian hobby	Male	200 grams	5 grams	Leg	1
Wedge-tailed eagle	Female	3900 grams	9 grams	Leg	1
Wedge-tailed eagle	Male	2900 grams	9 grams	Tail	2
Brown goshawk	Female	570 grams	7 grams	Tail	7
Brown goshawk	Male	320 grams	7 grams	Tail	3
Brown falcon	Female	600 grams	7 grams	Tail	2
Brown falcon	Male	490 grams	7 grams	Tail	2

* Tail-mounted transmitters resulted in fewer problems being experienced. Two of the goshawks released with leg-mounted transmitters became entangled in vegetation and had to be euthanized due to leg damage.

Table 4.3.5 Transmitters used on raptors both in the falconry and in the rehabilitation context.

Species	Sex	Weight	Transmitter weight	Falconry bird	Rehab/ research	Mounting
Peregrine	Male	650	6 grams	Yes		Tail
Peregrine	Female	980	12 grams		Yes	Harness mount
Peregrine	Female	880	7 grams		Yes	Tail
Peregrine	Male	600	7 grams		Yes	Leg
Peregrine	Female	870	7 grams		Yes	Tail
Peregrine	Female	850	9 grams		Yes	Tail
American kestrel	Female	150	4 grams	Yes		Neck mounted
Australian kestrel	Female	146	5 grams		Yes	Tail
Australian kestrel	Female	150	5 grams	Yes	Yes	Harness mount
Mauritius kestrel		-	5 grams		Yes	Harness mount
Merlin	Male	110	4 grams	Yes	Yes	Tail
Little falcon	Male	190	5 grams		Yes	Tail
Saker falcon	Both	-	15 grams		Yes	Harness mount
Saker falcon	Female	1000	9 grams	Yes		Tail
Gyr falcon	Female	1900	9 grams	Yes		Tail
Lanner falcon	Female	650	5 grams	Yes	Yes	Tail
Brown falcon	Male	520	7 grams		Yes	Tail
Aplomado falcon	Female	400	5 grams		Yes	Tail
Prairie falcon	Female	790	8 grams	Yes		Tail
Golden eagle	Female	4100	10 grams	Yes		Tail
Golden eagle	Female	-	15 grams	Yes		Harness mount
Verreaux's eagle		- -	15 grams		Yes	Harness mount
African hawk eagle	Female	-	9 grams	Yes	Yes	Tail mount
Red tailed hawk	Female	1000	9 grams	Yes		Leg mount
Ferruginous hawk	Female	1200	12 grams		Yes	Harness mount

4.4 RADIO TRACKING TROUBLE-SHOOTING

While the concept of radio tracking is ridiculously simple, the practice can be riddled with potential problems. Metal objects, water, dense vegetation, hills or other irregular terrain, and power lines all interfere with transmitter signals. The subject being radio tracked may be only a few hundred meters away and yet appear to be many kilometers away due to interference. If one is not careful, he can end up driving for miles only to find nothing. A degree of common sense assists in radio tracking, e.g., finding a high point or a hill will help in locating a good signal. It would be futile to attempt to locate a raptor if the bird is in one gully and the tracker is in another with a hill in between. Before any transmitter is used, both the transmitter and receiver should be checked for performance.

1. Check the frequency setting. On occasion, the set frequency may drift.

2. Check the range in open country and then in wooded country.
3. Check the receiver/co-axial cables/battery power. Most of the commercially available tracking devices are sealed units with a sealed battery. If any problems develop with the transmitter, it will have to be sent back to the manufacturer. Therefore, first make sure the problem is actually with the transmitter itself, and not the receiver!

As mentioned above, there are many things that can interfere with a transmitter signal, and the strength of that signal will wax and wane accordingly. Fences and large power lines can distort a signal, often giving the impression that a bird is closer than it actually is. When interference is experienced, it is important to determine where one is in relation to the probable cause of the interference. This allows one to move away from the problem and attempt to reestablish the signal.

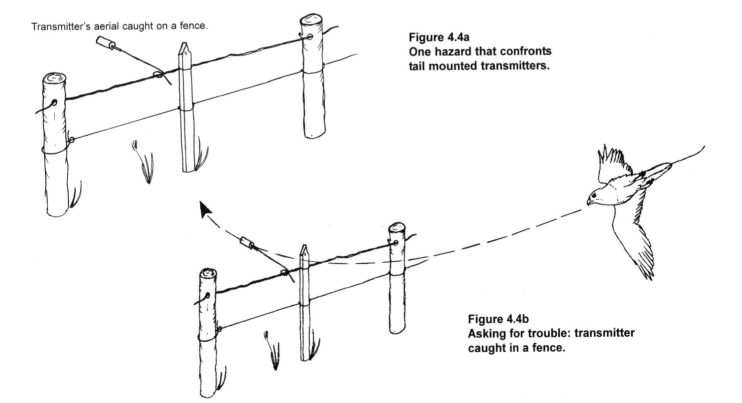

Transmitter's aerial caught on a fence.

**Figure 4.4a
One hazard that confronts
tail mounted transmitters.**

**Figure 4.4b
Asking for trouble: transmitter
caught in a fence.**

4.5 RADIO TRACKING GUIDELINES

Locating the transmitter

1. Check the frequency settings before and during a search. One can easily knock or alter the settings unknowingly, particularly during a strenuous hike over rugged terrain.
2. Keep the aerial elements parallel to the ground.
3. Listen carefully to the signal while slowly turning in a circle. The signal should fade as one moves away from the general direction of the transmitter.

4. If no signal is received, the operator should move 100 m (330 ft.) and try again.
5. Search for signals every 100 meters, by holding the aerial as high as possible or finding a high point. The signal waves are only received by a direct line-of-sight from the transmitter.
6. If there is a great deal of noise interference from vehicle traffic or wind, use a pair of head phones. Keep in mind that the signal will not be in stereo unless one has a stereo input plug for the headphones.
7. When receiving a very strong signal from a variety of locations, turn the gain on the receiver down and turn in a circle. Mark down where the best reception is coming from and follow that. A tracker who attempts to work with the receiver volume at its peak will be unable to discern any signal variation.

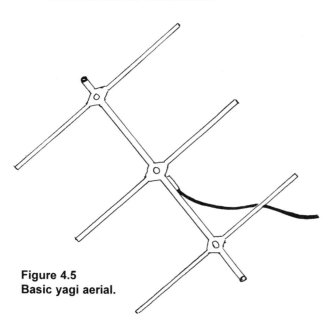

Figure 4.5
Basic yagi aerial.

Obtaining a topographical map of the area will allow the tracker to pick out all the higher elevations, thus facilitating the search. If a bird is perching on a fence post in a gully and the tracker is on the other side of a hill, he will not receive a signal, or if he does, it will be muffled, distorted, or just plain confusing.

4.6 POSSIBLE COMPLICATIONS

Standard falconry transmitters do not have a sealed battery. In such units, the batteries are removable. Thus, water can seep into the battery compartment and either corrode the contacts or short out the entire unit. These transmitters can be sealed with a bit of electrical insulation tape to pre-vent the possibility of corrosion. It is also vital to check the batteries before placing them in the transmitter. In addition, the contacts on the transmitter should be cleaned before it is attached to the bird.

Electric fences can short out a transmitter, particularly if the aerial protrudes for any distance beyond the tail tip; trimming the aerial is an option which might reduce the risk, but it will also cause some loss in receiving range, making it necessary for the tracker to be even closer to the transmitter in order to receive a good signal.

Sudden battery failure is not uncommon in receivers. Having a plug that will fit into the cigarette lighter of a vehicle will prevent the operator from becoming stuck with the combination of a dead receiver and bird close at hand. Alternatively, one can keep spare batteries for the receiver, if it is a unit in which the batteries can be replaced. Some receivers have a sealed, rechargeable nickel-cadmium battery which cannot be changed, so proper efforts should always be made to conserve battery power.

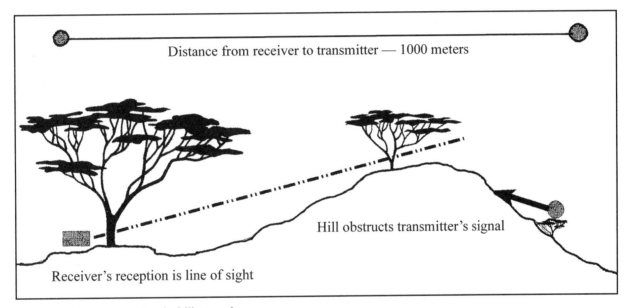

Figure 4.6 Radio tracking in hilly terrain.

4.7 BANDING (RINGING) FOR RELEASE

Aluminum or stainless steel bands that are numbered are often used to identify raptors that are being released. Color-coded and numbered bands have been used on peregrines released in urban environments, allowing the identification of individual birds seen perching. I consider that bands in general have limitations. The color-coded bands often become soiled, faded, or scratched, which makes reading them through a telescope very difficult. The stainless steel numbered bands have the same problem; additionally, they require the bird to be in the hand before it can be accurately identified. Banding for release is not an efficient method of gauging the success or survival of released birds, and one can only expect a 3% band return. Hawks that are banded and subsequently die in thick bush will never be found. Banding can be useful, but one should never rely upon bands as a means of gauging his success in the rehabilitation field.

Figure 4.7a *(above)* **Young peregrine falcon being banded in nest before release.** *Photo: David Hancock*

Figure 4.7b *(left)* **David Hancock banding a bald eagle prior to release.** *Photo: David Hancock*

4.8 THE FAILED RELEASE

This is a subject not often broached, but every rehabilitator will probably at some stage end up with a bird being returned because it did not cope effectively in the wild. Birds that are tame hacked, wild hacked, or simply released may end up back at the rehabilitation center with additional injuries, or in an emaciated state. In some cases, the birds may have been caught killing poultry or other livestock. Each returned bird should be re-assessed upon re-admittance, and consideration given to why it did not cope effectively and how the problem can be remedied. It is sometimes difficult to look at these cases objectively and make proper decisions. The longer a bird is under captive care, the harder it will ultimately be for it to survive unsupported in the wild. Euthanasia is an option that should not be overlooked or quickly dismissed for sentimental reasons. Or perhaps the individual bird in question would be better suited for use in an educational display or captive breeding project.

CHAPTER FIVE
THE CAPTIVE RAPTOR

5.1 MANAGING THE TRAINED RAPTOR

The subject of managing a captive raptor is comparatively straightforward. It involves keeping the bird in an environment that is conducive to maintaining its good health. The conditions under which it is kept, the equipment that is used to keep it tethered, the food it is fed, and the perches that are supplied are all part of the management regime. The task begins immediately when a bird is taken up for training, whether the reason is for falconry, demonstrations, or rehabilitation.

5.2 BEAK CARE

General appearance

Overgrown beaks and damaged feathers are visible imperfections, often noticed by observant visitors, and should not be tolerated. Most visible imperfections can be prevented or rectified. Overgrown beaks are often caused by soft food. Feeding a constant diet of day-old chickens to a raptor invariably results in an overgrown upper maxilla that is vulnerable to cracking, chipping, and splitting.

Falcon species, which have a tomial tooth, are particularly susceptible to this problem. Many zoos with extensive raptorial collections feed their birds a manufactured diet.

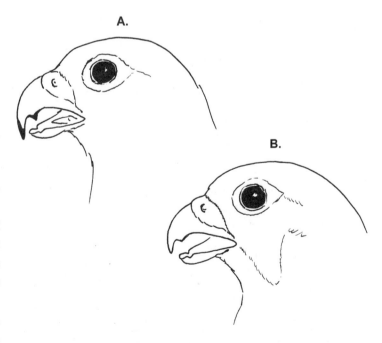

Figure 5.2 This bird has had the beak length reduced and filed (B).

Such artificial diets may be well-balanced in terms of containing all the bird's daily mineral and vitamin requirements. They do not, however, give the raptor an opportunity to tear and pull, which serves in the wild to prevent excessive beak growth. Without this natural check on their growth, the beaks of captive raptors may soon become overgrown. The inclusion of pigeon wings, rabbit forelegs, and chicken heads (see Table 5.2.1) in its diet will assist in keeping a raptor's beak neat and trim. It is important that the rehabilitator knows what a normal beak looks like, in order to determine whether remedial action needs to be taken. Those who are unsure of the proper appearance of the beak should examine photos of raptors with normal beaks.

Table 5.2.1 Daily diet for some raptors in ZOOS (Richard Naisbitt)

Species	Mon.	Tues.	Wed.	Thurs	Fri.	Sat.	Sun.
Kestrel	Mouse	Mouse	Mouse	pigeon wing	Mouse	Mouse	Mouse
Grey goshawk	Weaner rat	Chicken head	Weaner rat	Pigeon wing	Weaner rat	Weaner rat	Weaner rat
Brown falcon	Weaner rat	Weaner rat	Weaner rat	Pigeon wing	Weaner rat	Weaner rat	Weaner rat
Black falcon	Weaner rat	Chicken head	Weaner rat	Weaner rat	Weaner rat	Weaner rat	Weaner rat
Peregrine	Quail	Chicken head	Weaner rat	Quail	Weaner rat	Weaner rat	Weaner rat
Prairie falcon	Quail	Chicken head	Weaner rat	Quail	Weaner rat	Weaner rat	Weaner rat
Lanner falcon	Quail	Chicken head	Weaner rat	Quail	Weaner rat	Weaner rat	Weaner rat
Golden eagle	Rabbit head	½ rabbit	Quail	Marrow bone	Adult rat	Adult rat	Starve day
Tawny eagle	Rabbit head	½ rabbit	Quail	Marrow bone	Adult rat	Adult rat	Starve day
Bald eagle	Whole fish	Marrow bone	Quail	Adult rat	Adult rat	Adult rat	Starve day
Snake eagle	Adult rat	Marrow bone	Quail	5 day-old chickens	Adult rat	Adult rat	Starve day
Booted eagle	Adult rat	Rabbit hindleg	½ quail	3 day-old chickens	Chicken head	Adult rat	½ quail
Giant eagle owl	Adult rat	Rabbit hindleg	Adult rat	Quail	Chicken head	½ quail	2 mice
Barking owl	Weaner rat	Weaner rat	Weaner rat	½ rabbit	Rabbit foreleg	Weaner rat	Weaner rat
Barn owl	Weaner rat	Weaner rat	Weaner rat	Weaner rat	Rabbit foreleg	Weaner rat	Weaner rat
Scops owl	Mouse	Mouse	Pigeon wing	Day-old chicken	Chicken head	2 mice	Mouse
Boobook owl	Mouse	Mouse	Day old chicken	Pigeon wing	Chicken head	2 mice	Mouse
Wood owl	2 mice	2 mice	2 day-old chickens	Pigeon wing	Chicken head	2 mice	Mouse
Fishing owl	200 gram fish	Quail	Quail	200 gram fish	Chicken head	Quail	Quail
Coopers hawk	Weaner rat	Weaner rat	Weaner rat	Quail	Rabbit head	Weaner rat	Weaner rat
Sharp shinned hawk	Mouse	Mouse	Quail head and neck	Day old chicken	2 mice	2 mice	Quail breast
Turkey vulture	Adult rat	Adult rat	Rabbit head	Rabbit head	½ rabbit	Adult rat	Starve day
King vulture	Adult rat	Adult rat	Rabbit head	Rabbit head	½ rabbit	Adult rat	Starve day
White back vulture	Goat head	Adult rat	2 rabbit heads	Adult rat	½ rabbit	Adult rat	Starve day
Andean condor	Goat head	Adult rat	2 rabbit heads	2 adult rats	½ rabbit	Adult rat	Starve day

Mouse: Remember that not all mice weigh the same, this is a guide only, feed your raptors according to their weight.

Weaner rat: As for mice.

Chicken heads: This does not include the neck.

Pigeon wing: This does not include pectoral muscle or the coracoid but does include feathers.

Fish: Any species will do

½ rabbit: Hind quarters

5.3 FEATHER CARE

A raptor with damaged feathers will not only look unsightly, but will have its performance ability greatly reduced. Broken feathers can be repaired, but, as a rule, this problem can be prevented. Many trained hunting raptors break their feathers in the field through tackling prey they would not normally tackle in the wild. When a demonstration raptor damages or breaks its feathers, it is often a sign of bad management during training, or inappropriate housing, or both. Bating from a perch and colliding with or hanging from the wire mesh sides of an enclosure can cause feather damage. A raptor that sits back on its tail when it has food in its feet, or one that mantles wildly, will inevitably break tail feathers. Even on the glove, a raptor that mantles and bates will fray and break feathers. Perches that are placed too low, allowing the raptor's tail to rub against the floor, also contribute to feather deterioration. Stress bars formed during feather development will increase the risk of future feather breakages. Most of these problems can be prevented or avoided through a sensible management program during and after training.

All aspects of feather care are important. The use of tail guards during transportation and early training will assist in preserving tail feathers. Above all, a good diet during the period of feather development in young or molting birds ensures strong and healthy plumage capable of withstanding normal wear until the next molt. No raptor with damaged feathers can be safely released into the wild. All falconers, raptor handlers, or wildlife rehabilitators should be familiar with the basic procedures involved in caring for a raptor's feathers.

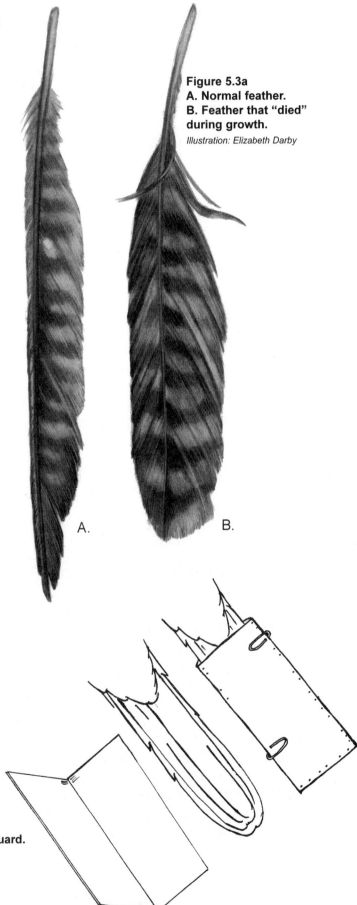

Figure 5.3a
A. Normal feather.
B. Feather that "died" during growth.
Illustration: Elizabeth Darby

A.   B.

Figure 5.3b Paper tail guard.

5.4 MOLTING

Almost all raptors begin their molt in the spring. Some individuals may start later, but generally, the molt, or the start of the molt, coincides with the advent of spring and increasing day length. Many falconers put their birds into a pen to complete the molt. This is a convenient practice, since the spring molt follows the end of the hunting season. Well-adjusted raptors that are being used in demonstrations can be flown through the molt as long as their flying weights are pushed up, i.e., the bird is being flown at the highest possible weight. The fear of stress fractures developing if a raptor is flown through the molt is often unfounded, particularly if the bird is well adjusted. I have flown many raptors through consecutive molts without any hunger/stress or fault bars developing in the feathers. Certainly wild birds which must forage for their sustenance cannot be expected to give up flying during the molt.

Since molting is a natural process which takes time to complete, the bird's life should go ahead as normally as possible. There are, of course, some exceptions to this general rule. Raptors that have damaged virtually all of their primary or tail feathers and are undergoing rehabilitation obviously need to be left in a secluded pen to complete the molt. In these situations, it is important to remember that the raptor will be totally wild and quite likely to thrash around the room if disturbed. Holding raptors in captivity on a long-term basis because of severely damaged feathers is one of my ongoing nightmares. To make matters worse, much of the feather damage I encounter could have been prevented by better management during rehabilitation. Bandaging wings of a molting raptor will usually damage the new, emerging feathers, but in certain instances this may prove to be the lesser of two evils. Putting on long-term tail guards immediately prior to or during the molt may exacerbate the problem of abnormal feather growth; it is wise to forego the tail guard in such situations.

5.5 REPAIRING FEATHERS

Damaged or broken feathers can be repaired in a number of ways. This process is known as "imping" and is comparatively simple, similar to the procedure used in pinning a bone. The correct method of imping is described in most falconry books, but a few extra hints should prove helpful to the raptor rehabilitator. Feathers cannot be mixed or substituted for any but the corresponding feather. For example, primary number nine of a male will only fit primary number nine of a male. Similarly, the feathers of a peregrine falcon cannot be used to repair those of a goshawk, although compatible species have been found for some raptors. The type, size, and shape of the feathers from the donor species must correspond to the same attributes in feathers being repaired. It should also be remembered that in raptors, the males are smaller than the females. Therefore, one cannot use a male primary to imp onto a female bird of the same species. On the other hand, the male primaries of one species may be suitable to substitute for the female feathers of a smaller species, or the feathers of a female of one species used to replace the feathers of a male of a slightly larger species.

The "imping pins" must be flexible, if possible, and are usually made from bamboo splinters that have been filed down until they are slightly smaller than the feather shaft's internal diameter. Alternatively, fiberglass splinters, perhaps from an old fishing rod, can be used; again, they should be filed down to meet the same requirements. In extreme cases, such as when the feather has snapped off near the base, the pin will need to be more of a plug, as the feather shaft this close to the follicle is hollow. The replacement shaft can first be glued, and then sewn, in place, to ensure that the repair will last.

While imping is a practical way of allowing a bird to carry on flying, I would offer a few words of caution. If the raptor is due for immediate release, or if it is undergoing rehabilitation and has more than four damaged primary or tail feathers that have been repaired, then release should be postponed. One may wonder why damaged feathers should be repaired in the first place. The reason is that each feather essentially supports its partner on each side; if one feather is broken, the ones next to it are exposed to higher risk of damage. The repaired feathers will protect the surrounding ones, thus preventing additional problems.

Many feathers break under strain that is abnormal, and some species are more susceptible to feather damage than are others. The flexibility of the feather is a major factor in determining whether a species is predisposed to feather damage. Peregrines, for example, are notoriously vulnerable to feather damage. They have stiff, almost rigid, feathers not designed to be bent or twisted. This, of course, is indicative of their attack strategies; very few peregrines will tackle prey on the ground, although the Australian peregrine is more likely to do so than other races. Black falcons, prairie falcons, sakers, and kestrels have very soft and pliable feathers. Although

feather breakages do occur in these species, this does not happen with the same frequency as in peregrine falcons. In some species of raptors, juveniles have longer, more pliable feathers than adults, designed to withstand the potential "knocks" of their training period, when flying is less than a perfect art. Regardless of feather texture, the incorrect housing of any species of raptor will still cause feather damage.

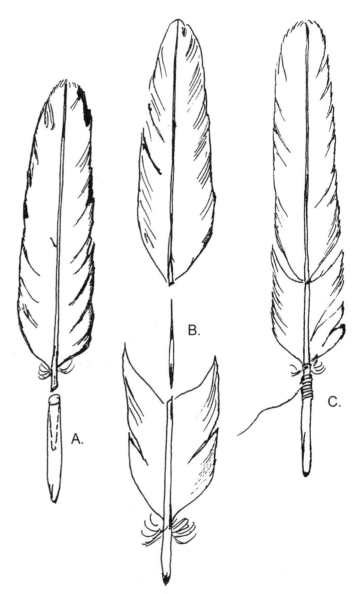

Figure 5 .5 Imping a feather.
A. Basal imp (inserting a feather into a feather stump).
B. Basic needle imp.
C. Basic and basal imp showing how to tie the basal area.

Table 5.5.1 Feather repair, compatible species (Richard Naisbitt)

Species	Sex	Compatible species	Imping material
Peregrine falcon	Male or Female	None	Fiber glass
Brown falcon	Male	Black falcon	Fiber glass
Brown falcon	Female	Black falcon	Fiber glass
Collared sparrowhawk	Female	Male Brown goshawk	Fiber glass
Collared sparrowhawk	Male	None	Fiber glass
Brown goshawk	Male	Female sparrowhawk	Fiber glass
Brown goshawk	Female	Female Grey goshawk	Fiber glass
Little falcon	Female	None	Fiber glass
Little falcon	Male	None	Fiber glass
European kestrel	Male	Female American kestrel	
American kestrel	Female	Male European kestrel	
Aplomado falcon	Female	Female New Zealand falcon	Fiber glass
Prairie falcon	Female	Female Lanner falcon	
Merlin	Male or	Female Eurasian hobby	Fiber glass
Gyr falcon	Male or Female	Saker falcon	Fiber glass
Lanner falcon	Male or Female	Barbary falcon	Fiber glass
Lugger falcon	Male or Female	Barbary falcon	Fiber glass
Red tailed hawk	Male or Female	Ferruginous hawk	Fiber glass
Little eagle	Female	Female Marsh harrier	Fiber glass
Little eagle	Male	Male Marsh harrier	Fiber glass
Bonelli's eagle	Male or Female	African hawk eagle	Fiber glass
Tawny eagle	Male or Female	Steppe eagle	Fiber glass
Golden eagle	Male or female	Bald eagle	Fiber glass
Wedge-tailed eagle	Male or female	None	Fiber glass

5.6 HOUSING TRAINED RAPTORS

There is the traditional way of housing a trained raptor, and then there are newer, safer methods. The classic mews still exist, but in name only, for the furniture inside has changed considerably. The old screen perch was dangerous, and liable to kill the occupant, or at least cause feather damage. Ideally, each raptor that is trained should be housed "loose" in a room free of protrusions, with plenty of ventilation, access to water, and comfortable, practical perches. If this is not possible, the use of shelf perches is the next best thing, particularly for falcons.

Tethering a raptor also has advantages. Aside from the fact that it prevents the bird from damaging its plumage or injuring itself, it allows the trainer to pick up the bird with a minimum of fuss.

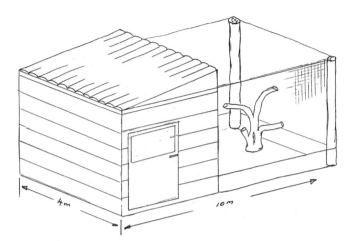

Figure 5.6a Basic mews.

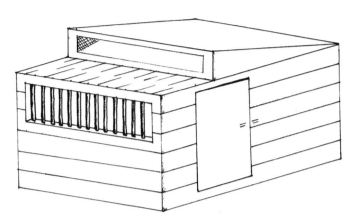

Figure 5.6b Enclosed mews.

Owls should be left free in a pen or room, as there is nothing more stressful for an owl than leaving it tethered to its perch in full view of eagles, falcons, and a myriad of other real or imagined threats. One should remember that even though an owl might be trained to fly in a demonstration during broad daylight, it still feels vulnerable when left exposed for long periods of time.

Housing options for raptors include:
a) Free lofting, being loose in a room.
b) Being tethered on shelf perches.
c) Being tethered on wide blocks (wide enough to allow the bird to lie down).

So what method of housing raptors works best? The only real proof exists in the occurrence or lack of injuries related to a particular type of housing. The free lofting of calm, well-adjusted raptors is preferable when adequate space is available. When this requirement cannot be met, then either shelf perches or wall-mounted bow perches are equally as good. The raptor should be offered the chance to lie down if it chooses. Wall-mounted bow perches should be the correct distance from the ground, which is high enough for the

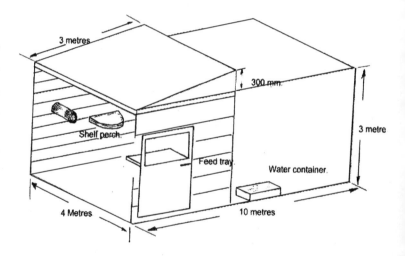

Figure 5.6c Holding pens for housing free lofted raptors.

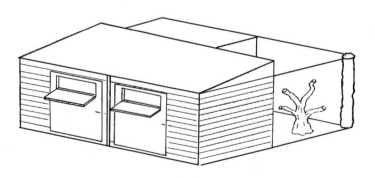

Figure 5.6d Dual pens for housing single orphans.

bird's tail to clear the floor, but low enough to allow the bird to hop off the perch and lie down.

It is always wise to design raptor accommodations in the most practical way possible. All of the rooms should be kept close together. They should have have good ventilation and allow for the penetration of natural light. It is always prudent to have a safety corridor, so that any bird which accidentally flies from its room when the door is opened cannot permanently escape. All doors should be clearly marked for accurate record-keeping, and have labels attached to indicate the current occupants. The overall design should make the journey from the rooms to the weathering area as short as is possible.

Eagles will kill other raptors. Leaving raptors in the weathering area while other, larger raptors are being flown is an open invitation to disaster. The weathering area should either be enclosed, or the birds removed to the safety of their respective rooms.

Each bird that is tethered, either in the weathering area or at night, must have at least 24 in. (60 cm) of free space on either side including any leaf extender. This prevents a bird which bates off the perch from reaching,

or being reached by, its nearest neighbors. In the weathering area, bow perches can be dragged along sand if they are mounted on a moveable base instead of being firmly pegged into the ground; some species will continuously bate at their neighbors, dragging their perches with them.

There are many methods of tethering raptors. The equipment used, including anklets (jesses), leashes, and swivels, will play a role in keeping trained birds out of trouble when they are tethered. Traditional jesses are cumbersome, often becoming twisted and tangled even when used in combination with the very best of swivels. Modern variations of this format are far preferable, very rarely twisting. In addition, the bird cannot undo them. The Arab style jesses and leash attachment are quite fine, but some birds learn how to undo them, or simply pick at them until they become undone, thereby posing a potential risk to other birds tethered close by. The best leather to use when making equipment like jesses is kangaroo hide that has been naturally tanned. It does stretch, so always pre-stretch it before fitting (see Chapter 10, Equipment, for further information). Aylmeri jesses are legally required in North America.

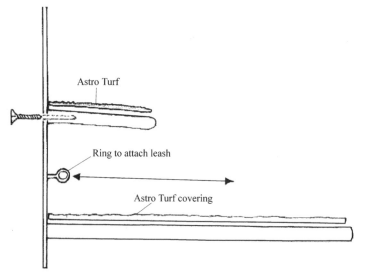

Figure 5.6e Basic shelf perch.

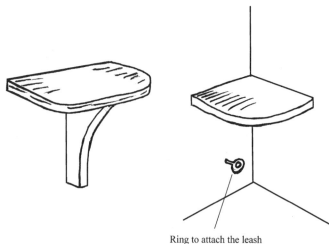

Figure 5.6f Shelf perches.

CHAPTER SIX
RAPTOR BEHAVIOR & TRAINING

6.1 MOTIVATION

Motivation is not a complex goal. Repeated failure to procure a meal will soon reduce motivation, while repeated success will increase motivation. Fitness and confidence all enhance motivation. Training a raptor is a matter of positive reinforcement, not negative reinforcement. If one examines the training process, breaking up each step and looking at the responses, it is easy to see how good motivation leads to desired results. The first jump to the glove is a positive step, reinforced by reward and repetition. It is vital that each training step be reinforced positively. The training process cannot progress properly unless each scheduled step has been achieved in its correct sequence. The raptor must be given clear messages. If called to the glove, it must respond in the desired manner, and not merely look at the trainer with an attitude that says "what do you want?"

To explain the reinforcement theory in basic terms, positive reinforcement of an action increases the likelihood that it will occur again, while negative reinforcement of an action decreases the chance that it will occur again. However, negative physical punishment does not work with raptors. Again, consider how a raptor behaves in the wild. When it launches an attack and is successful, the chances are it will use that same attack strategy again under similar circumstances. If, on the other hand, the raptor launches an attack and fails a number of times, the chances are that it will eventually abandon that particular strategy, or at least not use it under similar circumstances.

6.2 TRAINING METHODS

The basic steps for training a raptor haven't changed greatly over the centuries, but hopefully a change has taken place in our understanding of the processes behind training or the reasons why a bird will respond to certain visual or audio stimuli such as hand signals, whistles, or verbal calls. Traditional methods used a simple habituation technique to accustom the bird to being near a person or people. Today, falconers and rehabilitators are more aware of the importance of proper motivation, and modern conditioning techniques now reflect this awareness by being based on positive reinforcement (see Section 6.1).

For the newly acquired raptor, training must progress smoothly. The training process must be planned in advance, and each step must be fully accomplished before progressing further. The conditioning process goes through a series of steps; remember to shape each desired behavior before going on to the next step.

1. Glove training: This involves getting the bird used to the handler and the glove by carrying the bird on the glove.

2. Feeding on the glove: The bird learns to feed on the glove while the handler stands up and moves around.

3. Stepping to the glove: Teaching the bird to "come" to the handler by stepping forward onto the glove for food.

4. Flying to the glove: Progress from the bird stepping on to the glove to hopping on to it, followed by short and then long flights to the glove.

5. Introduction of the lure. The bird is now ready to begin fitness exercise and vertical flights.

Glove training

During each step of the training process, the handler must have a clear objective in mind. He should know what he plans to do and what response he wants to elicit from the raptor. This is vital for the bird undergoing rehabilitation.

Many wild raptors are reluctant to perch on the glove. They will either hang upside down or squat, which can make this step appear more difficult than it needs to be. The problem can be overcome by tethering the raptor to a perch in a quiet area where it can see the rehabilitator walking by, which should in time reduce its fear response to humans. It might prove useful to skip one day of feeding, and on the following day obliquely approach the bird and put a small piece of meat on the perch, after which the bird will start to associate the trainer with something positive. The reaction of the raptor to the rehabilitator will depend largely on its previous experience with people. Once its natural fear response has been dulled, the trainer can sit near the bird, with food offered on the perch; essentially, he is sneaking into the bird's world. Using this technique, a number of birds can be "conditioned" at the same time.

Feeding on the glove

Once the raptor is comfortable eating food from a perch with the trainer in close proximity, it should be ready to start feeding from the glove. It is hard to put a time frame on this part of training, but ten days should see the bird feeding with the trainer close at hand. Allowing the bird to take food offered in the gloved hand is a positive step toward getting it to step up onto the glove.

To sum up what has been accomplished so far:

First of all, the wild bird has been tethered in a safe area in close visual proximity to people. It has seen the trainer come and go with no adverse effects, only positive effects, such as leaving food. I recommend using a whistle just before approaching the bird with food, as this conditioned reinforcement will serve to announce the arrival of food, thus associating the sound of the whistle with something positive. Be careful not to mix this positive aspect with something negative, or the whistle may be misconstrued by the bird. Gradually, the handler has assimilated himself into the bird's world by slowly reducing the "flight distance." Initially, the bird would panic when seeing a person 65 ft. (20 m) away; now it allows the trainer to approach to within 6 ft. (2 m).

Once the raptor is feeding from the gloved hand, it is wise to start introducing it to environments other than the backyard or weathering area. However, one must continually watch for any signs of undue nervousness in order to ensure that the experience remains positive.

Stepping to the glove

Stepping to the glove for food is a natural progression which will normally happen without any undue mishaps. If the bird will step to the glove willingly, then many hurdles have been crossed and its fear responses have been suitably dulled. The most common difficulty that may arise at this stage is for the raptor to try to avoid stepping onto the glove by leaning forward to take the food. When confronted by this situation, the trainer must just persist. Eventually, the bird will respond in the desired way.

If all goes well, progress should be rapid, with the bird leaping to the glove as soon as food is offered. This is the secret, for in the wild a raptor of any species carries out a hunt by searching and then attacking; it must act instantly as prey does not wait to be caught. In a captive situation, this general behavior of a quick response must be encouraged by offering the glove and food for short periods. When the bird looks at the trainer, he should offer the food immediately; when it looks away, the food is removed until the bird looks again. The idea behind this is to remind the bird that the food is only present when initially offered. The bird must learn to act quickly when motivated. An aviary-bound raptor can become accustomed to seeing its food always lying in the same position on a ledge, and never moving. If the bird thinks that food is always available, it will become unmotivated. The offering and withdrawing of food will eliminate this problem.

Unmotivated behavior is not desirable in a trained raptor. An unmotivated, well-fed hawk is very selective. It will look briefly at the trainer and then look away. Each time the bird looks away, the moment has been lost for stimulating it or reinforcing a desired response. Within the brief time the bird is looking at the trainer, the trainer must offer motivation to the bird. He needs to increase the bird's attention span by improving its motivation to seek food. One way to improve motivation is to present the bird with novel situations during this period. It is a good idea to take the bird for a walk, then set it down on a low wall, tree stump, or fence post, from which it can then be called to the glove. This simple step can be adequately rewarded, and positively reinforced, with a small piece of food. I should, however, mention that the latter is often misinterpreted by trainers; holding a rabbit leg in your glove is not appropriate. Small pieces of meat, cut to the size of a thumb nail, are entirely adequate for this purpose, as ideally the bird should fly to your glove without seeing the food.

The creance

The distance from the perch to the glove can be gradually increased to induce a step and a flap until the bird is actually flying to the trainer. The use of a leash is good when starting to train the bird to jump to the fist or to a perch for food, but longer flights will require additional leash length. The creance is a length of nylon cord that is rolled on a reel by which it is held, with the required amount of line let out. One end is tied to the raptor's jesses and the other end remains attached to the reel. The trainer holds the line to add some drag, and to stop the bird from entering vegetation. One must always remember to secure the creance firmly to the reel and securely to the bird, and then hold the cord in his gloved hand with the reel at his feet. The hawk flying on a creance can feel the drag, and it will compensate for this by altering its flight pattern. When the line is removed, the drag is suddenly gone and the whole act of free flying takes on a new perspective.

Before the bird is flown, the creance should be checked for signs of wear and tear. It is a good idea to use a transmitter on any bird that is being flown on a creance. This enables the trainer to locate and retrieve the bird if the line breaks.

When the bird is flying to the glove consistently over a distance of 65 ft. (20 m), it can be flown free. However, there are few considerations that must be addressed before any bird is free flown.

1. Make sure the bird can cope with novel situations. What one doesn't want is a bird that has lurking unpredictable behavior and will only work within a familiar environment. The bird must learn that the reward can be expected no matter where it flies.

2. Make sure the bird is responding as soon as food is offered or following the trainer before he is ready to call. This indicates that the bird knows what is coming, and that it is comfortable with the trainer. If a lure is to be used, it can be introduced at this stage.

3. Alter the flying time, making it thirty minutes later, on the day of the bird's first planned free flight, and increase the bird's motivation by offering less food the day before.

There is no point in assuming the bird will come out of a tree on the first free flight. The only way one can be confident it will come out of a tree is through the knowledge that it has been properly trained to respond to the motivation offered. Do not try to call a bird down from a tree with the wind at its back and at a steep angle. Instead, move to an area where the bird will be flying into the wind at an angle that is easy for it to glide down. As the bird becomes more experienced and flight competent, it will work out the easiest way to return to the trainer. However, the bird on its maiden free flight needs a less traumatic introduction to its future relationship with the trainer, who must be careful and considerate. For the raptor undergoing rehabilitation, its release viability can be assessed at this stage. If necessary, exercise regimes can be implemented to improve its fitness, flight competence, and foraging ability.

6.3 LURE TRAINING

Traditionally, falconers used the lure to retrieve certain species; today, many falconers, rehabilitators, and demonstrators use the lure as a matter of course. When the lure is used properly, it has an important place in the training and rehabilitation of raptors, especially for those at tame hack or those destined for demonstration work. It can serve to demonstrate a certain foraging style, improve a bird's flying ability, fitness, and footing, and improve basic prey capture skills. When necessary, the lure may be used to retrieve a bird. Lures come in various forms, from the leather pad to the legless rabbit or ornately crafted and painted leather ducks.

Figure 6.3 Leather lure with wings attached.

Various types of lures are suitable for use with different species. Naturally, the very aerial falcons work well to a swung lure which allows for their attack strategy. Most typical searchers, due to their foraging strategies, are not suited to lure pursuit flights; but some species, such as the red- tailed hawk, benefit from being exercised by using a dragged rabbit lure. The eagles, buzzards, and goshawks work better to a dragged lure, again following their natural attack strategies. Swinging the lure does require a certain degree of experience and learned coordination, and the only way to learn is by watching and practicing, always bearing in mind what the training process is intended to achieve.

It is essential for the trainer to consider the species, and plan the lure's use not only to match the bird's natural attack strategies, but to ensure that it enjoys a measure of success for its efforts. We have seen that a bird's behavior in the wild is replicated in captivity, and that a wild raptor chooses the best method of attack by experience; the more successful a

particular method, the more frequently it will be used and the greater the success the bird's efforts will generate. If the lure is seen either as something impossible to catch or as something very easily caught, the bird's behavior and attitude will swing from one extreme to the other, i.e., from totally ignoring the lure to chasing it lethargically, waiting for the trainer to let it drop.

The trainer should also take into account the weather conditions, which can complicate lure flying. Hot days with no wind will make flying to the lure incredibly difficult for falcons, and the trainer will invariably end up with the bird sitting in a tree. Cool days with a good breeze will offer more opportunity for the bird to perform at peak capacity.

6.3.1 Introducing the lure

It is always wise to make sure the raptor is flying to the glove competently before introducing the lure, as this ensures that any fear of the trainer is already dulled or eliminated. In many cases, the bird will simply look at the lure with a certain degree of confusion. Placing the raptor on a low perch and then dropping the lure close by it will encourage the bird to jump down and investigate; if there is a very obvious piece of food tied to the lure, the motivation to grab it will be greater. When this happens, the bird should be allowed to feed off the lure before being picked up. By offering another small piece of food in the glove, the trainer can make sure the bird lets go of the lure before he picks it up. An easy transference from the lure to the glove is desirable. The falcon, eagle, buzzard, or hawk should fly to both the glove and the lure. Although fast-flying falcons may be reluctant to slow down and land, they will do so if they are confident, and some will even come out of a stoop to land lightly on the glove. In time, the lure becomes a "bridge" or a "cue." The lure is swung, and the bird catches it and is fed; eventually, food can be left off the lure.

Chasing the ground lure.

Pursuing the aerial lure.

Throwing the lure.

Figure 6.3.1 Lure flights.

6.3.2 The dragged lure

For those species that take their prey on the ground, a dragged lure can be used. Introduction to a dragged lure should not differ to that of any other lure type. Hawks, buzzards, eagles, and some falcons can be conditioned to pursue a dragged lure. There are many wonderful "lure dragging" devices available that mechanically drag the lure using a reel. The lure line can be 660 ft. (200 m) long and set out around a number of obstacles to make the lure run an erratic course. This is also a great way to improve fitness in many species, and I have used this type of lure for peregrines, hawks, and eagles.

6.3.3 Lures and complications

The benefits of lures, when correctly used, have been referred to in Section 6.3, but complications can arise. The novice may find using a lure difficult, and the resultant problems will manifest themselves in either a poor response by the bird to the lure, or in aggression toward the lure, and later, toward the glove or even toward the trainer. The true hawks, the larger buzzards, and the eagles are very prone to developing aggressive behavior toward the trainer. Mantling, biting, and footing are all undesirable traits that can result from poor handling at some stage.

Other problems are created by tying food to the lure. The bird may tear the food off the lure and carry it away, or it may become possessive over the lure. In this instance, the bird will refuse to give up the lure, particularly if it sees the trainer as a competitor. To compound the problem, this belief will be reinforced if the trainer tears the lure away from the bird. Large eagles that have a long period of dependency may become very possessive over their hard caught, synthetic meal, and for the safety of the trainer, the eagle should not view him as a competitor for the food.

The single orphaned eagle poses a greater problem, and as previously noted, the faster it learns to fly and becomes semi-independent, the better for both the bird and the trainer. In the rehabilitation context, particularly for raptors destined to be tame hacked, the lure can be introduced much earlier. Young eagles, hawks, buzzards, or falcons can be called across a backyard lawn to the lure well before they can fly.

Another problem, particularly applicable to falcons, is having the bird become lure-bound. The consequences are equally serious for both the demonstrator and falconer. In this instance, the falcon has invariably learned that it is easier to wait for the lure to drop, rather than give chase. Such a bird will ignore potential prey and seek the nearest perch as soon as it is cast off the glove. Preventing a bird from becoming lure bound can be accomplished through the use of common sense, as can all bad or undesirable behaviors (see Section 6.4). If a falcon waits for the lure to be dropped after it has taken to the nearest perch on release or casting off, then one must go back to the drawing board and start the re-education slowly. Drop the lure only when the falcon is in the air. This may be time consuming, but take each step one at a time and the goal will eventually be achieved.

Problems can also develop if the falcon is unfit, in which case it cannot sustain long, arduous lure pursuits. The overworked bird will rest in a tree or on any perch. Throwing the lure out at this stage and letting the bird secure it will only re-enforce this behavior, as will throwing the lure out and pulling it away as the bird leaves the perch. The solution is not to let the bird perch in the first place. Keep the exercise sessions short by starting with a low number of passes and building the number up slowly over several days. In addition, the bird should be allowed to use any wind or lift it can find to make things easier. If the falcon does perch, the trainer should go and sit

Illustration: Elizabeth Darby

under a tree and wait until it leaves of its own accord, then call it down once it is in the air.

Lack of response to the lure, or a slow response time, is another problem sometimes encountered when working with a lure. In much the same way the bird may refuse to respond to the glove when offered, it may refuse to respond to the lure when offered. This usually results from calling repeatedly, swinging the lure, and then dropping it, regardless of whether the bird is watching or not. In essence, the trainer is showing the bird that the lure, like the glove, will be there no matter what happens.

In conclusion, it is important to note that when using a lure, the trainer must be honest and consistent. He should never use the lure to entice a bird down from a tree and then retract the reward, i.e., renege on the offer of food. If any of the problems discussed exist, the trainer should go back and re-evaluate what he has done, in order to correct any mistakes he has made. He should then start afresh, eliminating all the vices he has inadvertently created.

6.4 UNWANTED BEHAVIOR

Suppose a falcon has been flying for three weeks and has chased the lure with wonderful persistence. The trainer becomes overconfident and begins to overdo the training. The falcon proves to be less fit that he thought, and one day becomes tired and lands in a tall tree. The trainer throws the lure on the ground and waits; eventually the bird comes down and takes its meal. The next day, the same scenario is repeated. The bird leaves the glove and lands in a tree, only this time the day is hot and there is no wind. The trainer waits a few minutes and then throws out the lure. As the falcon leaves the tree, he pulls the lure up to start swinging. The falcon makes one pass and lands again. This time the trainer leaves the lure on the ground, the falcon lands and is fed. Very soon your falcon lands every time the trainer casts it off the glove. In this instance, the bird has succeeded in training the trainer. It will not come down until the lure is thrown out and left.

The trainer is now faced with a dilemma. He has inadvertently taught the bird an incorrect and undesirable behavioral pattern, which must be altered before the next step in the training process is undertaken. One possible solution is to change the flying area and start again, focussing on the desired behavior. If one is unable to move to another location, then the only option is to enforce the desired behavior. This can be accomplished by casting the falcon off the glove and watching it carefully; if it heads for a tree, it must be called immediately, either by shouting or using a whistle. When the bird turns in response to the call, the lure should be thrown out. This process must be repeated until the falcon is watching the trainer constantly. It can be allowed to do one circuit, and then two, and so on.

Other problems occur early in the training process. For example, calling a bird to your raised fist repeatedly without any reaction from the bird enforces a poor response. The trainer is, in effect, telling the bird that he will be there for at least ten minutes, and that when it finally decides to fly to him it will still be fed. This discourages the quick response behavior that is so necessary for a bird which is to be released eventually into the wild. If the bird does not respond immediately, the food should be put away. The trainer should wait for about ten seconds, move a few meters, and then try again.

Figure 6.4 Screaming for food.

The message he is now giving is that "the food is available for a few seconds only," rather than "I will be here all day, so take your time." As stated previously, locating prey in the wild might take some time, but assessing the prey for vulnerability must take only a few seconds, and action is often instantaneous. The objective of training is to transfer this behavior to the demonstration.

Screaming for food is another behavioral problem which is more likely to occur with falcons than true hawks (accipiters). In many cases screaming, or calling for food, is a created problem, often reinforced through bad handling. The reason the falcon is screaming is simply that it wants to be fed and has become dependent upon the trainer. The longer the bird remains dependent, the longer it will scream. Dropping a young raptor's weight in the early stages of training can often cause screaming, particularly if the bird has been removed from its natural parents before the imprinting process has been completed. In this instance, the falcon simply transfers its natural begging responses onto the trainer, who becomes its surrogate parent.

The only solution to the problem of a raptor screaming for food is to allow it to achieve its independence. However, this is a problem that usually can be prevented. The handler should feed the developing falcon as much as it can eat, and make sure the bird can feed itself, with an abundant food supply being left for it to feed on at leisure. Hand feeding the young raptor simply reinforces the perception of the trainer as a parent figure. Remember, hacking can help in these situations, but many institutions cannot afford that luxury. If a bird has been pushed straight from basic training into a flight demonstration without learning the skills required to become independent, then screaming will continue for a long period.

Aggression is another unnecessary behavior that is rarely discussed. It is vital to understand aggressive behavior in correct context by identifying its cause. Aggression may be associated with territoriality or food. Aggression linked to territory is often displayed by imprinted eagles or large buzzards, and may be recognized by removing the bird from its home environment. If the aggression suddenly stops until the bird familiarizes itself with its new surroundings, then territoriality can be deemed to be the cause of its aggression. All of the eagles I handle show markedly different behaviors when moved out of the area in which they normally work. Eagles eventually choose the trainer with whom they will work, and inevitably it is the person who has handled them the most. It is very difficult to deal with situations where an eagle repeatedly lunges at or tries to intimidate a trainer. Force or other negative reinforcement will not work; it either provokes fresh attacks or instills a fear of the person who has reacted with force. It is often wise not to feed eagles off the glove—particulary imprints.

Food-linked aggression is more evident if the raptor has been hand raised or is being trained before some degree of independence has been attained. Problems associated with this type of aggression have been discussed in the preceding paragraphs and in Section 6.3.3, Lures and complications. This problem may also develop in some species that are natural pirates, i.e., birds which steal food from other raptors. Some examples are whistling kites, tawny eagles, and fishing eagles; these birds will be more inclined to try to intimidate the handler into giving them food. Reference should also be made here to mantling on the glove, which should not be confused with aggression; this is a defensive behavior and represents a different issue altogether.

In summary, captive raptors can display many undesirable traits that are largely based on their natural behavior and inadvertently exacerbated by poor handling. Behavioral problems can be rectified if time is taken to correctly identify the cause and then take appropriate remedial action.

6.5 Weight management during training

As weight management is a complex issue, in this section I intend to outline its basic principles and offer guidelines only. Managing a raptor's weight is critical during its training and afterward, when it is accustomed to working within a certain routine. The common attitude toward an unresponsive bird is to drop its weight in an effort to refocus its attention on the trainer and what he offers in terms of food. However, this attitude ignores the fact that what is really required is motivation. As food is the only incentive with which the trainer can effectively motivate a bird, it must be used positively and wisely. Good weight management means having a raptor with a healthy appetite, not one that is desperately hungry.

Sensible weight management is an integral part of the initial phases of training when the handler is 'manning' the bird. The bird's weight should be at the exact point where its desire to eat, its appetite, is greater than its fear response toward its handler and its new environment. The bird should then let down its guard enough to accept food from the trainer and eat with the trainer in close visual proximity. Remember, in the wild a bird may be a certain weight and frequently hunt, but when first placed in captivity, even at that same weight, it will not immediately respond to food when offered, as its fear responses override its appetite.

If a raptor can be considered overweight or fat (I use the term loosely), obviously it will be unresponsive toward the trainer, and progress will be difficult to make. Before training starts, it is vital that a new bird be weighed and the weight recorded. One can then calculate how much weight the bird will need to lose in order to improve its motivation. Once a raptor is responding, there is no reason to keep it at a low weight, as it needs food for energy and to build fitness and muscle mass.

In certain cases, the loss of weight will not accelerate training. I am particularly referring to those raptors which are more fearful than normal and therefore respond very slowly. One should never forget that many raptors undergoing rehabilitation and subsequent treatment have their natural fear responses enhanced through the repeated capture and restraint required by this process. During their early days in captivity, the "forced manning" may be the only time they see the trainer. In consequence, the trainer soon becomes associated with such treatment, which to the raptor represents a bad experience. In this situation, attention should not be focussed on weight loss, but on slowly breaking down the bird's fear responses, so that it is comfortable with the trainer nearby. If a raptor is fearful or generally stressed, one should address its fear before attempting to drop its weight.

The weight loss and subsequent gain by a juvenile peregrine falcon during the first fifteen days of training are illustrated in Figure 6.5a. This bird had suffered a fractured ulna and had been in care for 28 days prior to being admitted for rehabilitation. Days 0–10 were good in terms of the bird being receptive to the food offered on the glove. As the bird was responding well, there was no reason to keep its weight down, so from Day 13 onward, its fitness was built in conjunction with reinforcing the conditioned behavior of flying to the handler for food (vertical flights). It is vital that a raptor's weight be slowly restored to the point it was at prior to the start of training.

Then, as fitness improves and muscle mass increases, the bird's weight can be pushed up even further.

There are several factors to consider in regard to a raptor's weight. The weight variation between different species must obviously be taken into account. Even more important is the variation among individuals of the same species. Not only are females usually bigger than males, but further variations may be encountered depending on the area from which the bird originated, resulting from sub-specific differences or the quality of the habitat. The size of a bird is a factor which influences its metabolic rate. Even small variations in weight are critical where small raptors are concerned. In addition, the weather and available natural light will affect a bird's weight loss and its resultant degree of hunger. The rate of digestion decreases during the night, and fluctuates during the day according to weather and light conditions.

A falcon weighed in the morning can lose up to 20 grams by the afternoon. Figure 6.5b shows a male peregrine falcon's weight loss

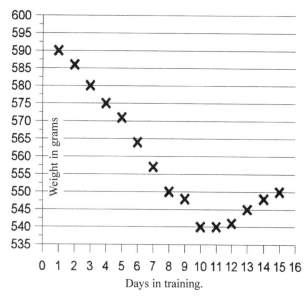

Figure 6.5a Peregrine falcon's weight loss and gain during training.

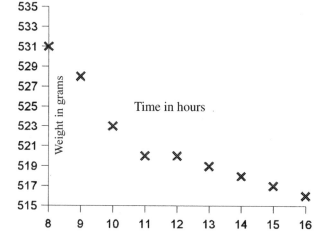

Figure 6.5b Male peregrine falcon's weight loss over 8 hours.

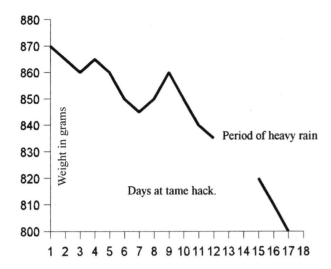

Figure 6.5c Weight loss of a released female peregrine.

over a period of eight hours. From 8:00 A.M. to 4:00 P.M., it lost 15 grams. As this bird was tethered to its perch and not active, one can easily imagine how much weight it might have lost if it had been subjected to a heavy work-out and had not been fed.

When training a raptor, it is essential that one understands the different calorific values of food and how the bird uses this food in relation to its workload. Without this knowledge, weight management will be irrelevant. The relationship between energy requirements and food intake is illustrated in Figure 6.5c, which shows how much weight a large female peregrine falcon lost over seventeen days during a preliminary release.

This falcon was called to the lure every day and then weighed on a portable pair of electronic scales after temporary jesses were fitted. No supplementary feeding took place, and the only food offered was on the lure. On Days 7–10, the falcon regained some lost weight. During this period, she was observed feeding on a dead lamb, portions of which she cached. Periods of heavy rainfall hampered her subsequent hunting forays, and she again lost weight. Her weight decline was significant after she had lost 30 grams, and within 17 days she lost a total of 70 grams. The bird's food consumption was clearly inadequate, as she did not replace the energy she expended.

A program of supplementary feeding was then inaugurated, and three months later the falcon was independent. Her last recorded weight was 900 grams.

Before ending this section, several aspects of weight management should be clearly understood. First, lack of a response to offered stimuli is not always due to a weight problem. It can be related to mixed messages being sent or received; the raptor does not understand what it is supposed to do. Second, a raptor's weight must not be permanently kept low; a safe margin should always be kept. Third, a raptor's weight should be pushed up over time, taking into account the weather conditions and what the bird did during the routine, and noting when it becomes unresponsive or slow to respond. It is always a good idea to weigh the food being given to the raptor and then monitor its weight increase or decrease. Fourth, keeping accurate weight records is vital if a bird is to be kept in a fit, healthy condition. Fifth, weight management is not about starvation. A raptor can do nothing if it is starving. Weight management involves getting the best response from a bird at its healthiest and highest possible weight.

6.6 IMPROVING AND MAINTAINING FITNESS

Fitness can be defined as a bird's ability to carry out set exercise routines without succumbing to exhaustion. It can only be developed if the raptor is in good health at the start. Raptors that have been forced to rest for long periods, either because of a molt or injury, will need to have their fitness built up over a period of time. There is little difference between the fitness requirements of a bird undergoing rehabilitation or one that is expected to perform well in a demonstration or when hunting. Many of the failures exhibited by falconry birds in the field can be attributed to a lack of fitness, and many demonstration birds unable to give a good account of themselves are equally unfit.

When considering fitness, it is interesting to observe the young raptor in the nest. Its initial exercise consists of wing flapping while clinging to the edge of the nest. This is followed by a first flight that may be nothing more than a glide. Prolonged flight comes after a few weeks of practice, then play periods with siblings or parents further improve fitness and flight skills. The young bird's fitness is built gradually over a lengthy period where flight is not inhibited by tethering, flight pens, or small enclosures. At ten weeks of age, the wild-fledged raptor is months ahead of the aviary-fledged bird in terms of flight skill and fitness.

It is crucial to keep this point in mind when training a raptor for demonstration or release. Ideally, the trainer should get the young bird into the air as soon as is physically possible. Prior to its first free flight, basic fitness can be built through the simple exercise of repetitive flights to the glove, either vertically or at a steep angle or gradient. This exercise will not only build fitness, but will also reinforce the basic message of what is expected from the bird when it is called.

It is difficult to enhance a bird's fitness unless proper care has been taken with initial training procedures. Close contact methods, such as lure flying or flying to the glove, require a good degree of trust; if this has not been established, then fitness training will be futile. The differences between encouraged flight and forced flight have been discussed in section 2.5, Rehabilitation techniques. If exercise is encouraged rather than forced, it is possible to get more out of a bird.

There are four basic exercise regimes used for trained raptors or raptors that need to have their fitness improved before release. These include 4 m (12 ft.) vertical flights, 15 m (50 ft.) gradient flights, 50 m (165 ft.) level flights, and lure flying. Improving the fitness of an unfit raptor is a slow process. Short-cuts, or attempts to speed up the process, will inevitably lead to failure. There is no point in reducing a raptor's weight and then increasing its workload; this will result only in an exhausted bird. It offers absolutely no benefit in improved performance. One must always begin with basic exercises, and then follow the regimes recommended for the particular species in table 6.6.1.

Many of the exercise routines can be carried out in two sessions. The bird's initial attempts may be comparatively poor, but the sessions can be built up over ensuing weeks. It is always difficult to judge when the bird has had enough; a slow response time is one indication that the session should be brought to an end. It is always better to start off with a small number of passes and build up to a higher number. Targets which should be reached after four weeks of exercise are suggested in table 6.6.2.

4 meter vertical flights

This exercise can be used with virtually all species. The number of flights can be increased on a daily basis until the bird has achieved a pre-set target. It is often necessary to carry out the exercises in two parts, with a break in between.

15 meter gradient flights

Eagles benefit more from this type of exercise, which is in essence a combination of vertical and level flight.

50 meter level flight

Early training invariably involves some level flying. Many raptors try to avoid "working" when flying from point to point, particularly if the perches are high enough to allow the bird to glide. Heavy-bodied eagles benefit from this exercise, but only if the perches are 3 ft. (1 m) off the ground; at this height, the bird cannot glide but has to work to keep in the air.

Lure Flight

This exercise serves a number of purposes, but is more applicable to those species which use some form of direct flight when attacking prey. Kestrels can very effectively fly a pole swung lure. Brown falcons are often not sufficiently motivated to persist in a lure flight. For many species, the use of a hand or pole swung or dragged lure is excellent. Others, like the harriers, are limited to one or two pursuits at the ground lure, but this can be compensated for by using a vertical flight exercise afterward. A motorized dragged lure is ideal for ground lure work as one can increase the lure's speed at will, making it harder for the bird to catch. Each attempt can be interspersed with periodic breaks. A falcon will be more persistent when chasing the lure, due to its natural pursuit tendencies. A goshawk will behave differently, and be less inclined to repeat the exercise in quick succession. Success will breed success. The trainer should

Table 6.6.1 Recommended exercise regimes

Species	4 m vertical flights	15 m gradient flights	50 m level flights	Lure flying
Peregrine falcon	Yes			Yes (aerial lure)
Black falcon	Yes	Yes		Yes (aerial lure)
Little falcon	Yes			Yes (aerial lure)
Kestrel	Yes		Yes	Yes* (aerial lure)
Brown falcon	Yes	Yes		Yes* (aerial lure)
Goshawk	Yes			Yes (dragged lure)
Cooper's hawk	Yes			Yes (dragged lure)
Sparrowhawk	Yes			Yes (dragged lure)
Golden eagle	Yes	Yes	Yes	Yes (dragged lure)
Sea eagles/Bald eagle	Yes	Yes	Yes	Yes (dragged lure)
Hawk eagle	Yes	Yes	Yes	Yes (dragged lure)
Black kite			Yes	
Whistling kite			Yes	
Marsh harrier			Yes	Yes (dragged lure)
All owl species			Yes	

* Difficult to encourage pursuit of aerial lure as these species do not use aerial pursuit as primary attack strategy.

never allow the bird to fail consistently, for if this happens, all motivation will be lost.

A raptor's wild behavior should be examined when setting out exercise strategies. The attack distances and duration between attacks of various species of raptors are shown in table 6.6.3. It is vital that exercise regimes conform to the bird's natural method of attack. In the case of birds being rehabilitated, one must determine what they are required to do in the wild, and then plan the exercise accordingly. The same strategy can be applied to birds being flown in demonstrations or used for hunting in classical falconry.

Table 6.6.2 Exercise targets after four weeks

Species	4 m vertical flights	15 m gradient flights	50 m level flights	Lure flying
Peregrine falcon	60			80
Black falcon	60	30		80
Little falcon/Merlin	30			30
Kestrel	30		15	15
Brown falcon	60			50
Goshawk	60			6 (20–30 m)
Cooper's hawk	60			6 (20–30 m)
Sparrowhawk	40			6 (30 m)
Golden eagle	40	60	20	10 (50 m)
Sea eagles/Bald eagle	40	60	20	10 (50 m)
Hawk eagle	40	60	20	10 (50 m)
Black kite			15	
Whistling kite			15	
Marsh harrier			20	10 (50 m)
All owls			20 (forced flight)	

Table 6.6.3 Attack distances and duration between attacks

Species	Number of attacks	Distance to prey*	Successes	Time between attacks
Peregrine falcon	9	300 - 400 m	2**	10-25 minutes
Black falcon	18	500 - 800 m	3**	16 - 20 minutes
Little falcon	24	100 - 200 m	5***	5 - 15 minutes
Australian kestrel	14	20 m	12****	5 - 15 minutes
Brown falcon	8	5 - 15 m	7****	10 -20 minutes
Brown goshawk	4	20 - 30 m	1	15 -33 minutes
Collared Sparrowhawk	9	15 - 20 m	1	30 - 45 minutes
White-bellied sea eagle	6	300 - 500 m	1	20 - 30 minutes
Wedge-tailed eagle	1	1000 m	0	0

The duration between attacks is given as a time range
   *   The distance from the point where the attacks started to the location of the prey item was measured after the event.
  **   Starlings were caught in this instance.
 ***   This little falcon cached all but four of the unidentified birds caught.
****   Invertebrates were the prey in the case of the kestrel and the brown falcon.

6.7 CHOOSING THE RIGHT RAPTOR FOR A DEMONSTRATION

The primary purpose of a flight demonstration is to exhibit a raptor's natural range of behaviors. When selecting species for a flight demonstration, this purpose should be kept in mind. A flight demonstration must be a cohesive team effort with birds and trainers working together. Training a raptor to work within a routine and to perform in front of an audience is a challenge. Its first free flight, followed weeks later by its first appearance in a demonstration, can be daunting. The importance of choosing both the right species and the right individual bird cannot be over-emphasized.

What do various species have to offer as demonstration birds? First of all, one should consider the natural foraging strategies of a species and then envision these strategies in the demonstration situation, asking oneself if these behaviors can be reproduced in a rigid and confined environment. Under captive conditions it will be more difficult to display some species' abilities to good advantage, e.g., true hawks. Many wild raptors may use a number of attack strategies in one hunt; the glide attack may turn into a tail-chase, or when prey has taken cover, the hawk may use a glide attack again, or it may stalk its prey on foot through the undergrowth. Many of these tactics are not demonstrable during a short five minute display, so it is wise to stick with obvious and comparatively exciting strategies.

The most easily displayed foraging strategies are those that are attack strategies, e.g., an eagle or buzzard chasing a lure, a falcon stooping to a lure, or a sea eagle fishing. Searching strategies can also be displayed. Some of the owls can be encouraged to locate food using audio cues that emphasize the "search" component of foraging. It is obviously more educational to combine various species to illustrate different search and attack strategies

(see Tables 6.7.1 and 6.7.2, respectively) than simply using several species which have similar behavioral traits when foraging. Another demonstration technique that adds excitement is to have several raptors simultaneously exhibit the same or varied strategies so many viewers see what is happening.

The ideal demonstration raptor should be parent-reared (owls are the exception) with normal fear responses. Experience in the air is also vital. It is beneficial to fly the potential demonstration bird under a variety of conditions and in various locations before it is introduced to a more rigid demonstration. Traditional hacking is very useful in these circumstances. It does, however, depend on what style of demonstration is being planned. Many hand-raised raptors turn out to be unsuitable for flight displays due to incorrect hand-rearing or training. They exhibit a range of unwanted behaviors including screaming and aggression. Eagles are particularly dangerous if they are not properly trained, handled, and flown.

Sufficient space is vital if a good display is to be given; the more room available the better, depending upon the species and behaviors being demonstrated. Some of the owls only require a small area to show their skills. True hawks (Accipiters) are generally not suitable for use in public flight displays.

Many flight displays use a designated demonstration area, with the audience separated by discreet barriers, restricted from entering the "stage" where the performance takes place. This arrangement allows the raptors sufficient space in which to work and reduces any natural shyness on their part. If the audience is in close proximity, with no barriers, then the bird being flown needs to be totally at ease with people talking, moving, and applauding; it must regard the audience as part of its routine, and not as an intrusion.

Table 6.7.1 Demonstrable attack strategies and their effectiveness

Species	Attack strategy	Demonstrable	Method	Effectiveness
Peregrine	Stoop	Yes	Lure flying	Good
Small falcon (Merlin)	Tail-chase	Yes	Lure flying	Good
Kestrel	Hover /drop	Yes	Lure flying	Good
Brown falcon	Glide attack	Yes	Lure flying	Poor
Lanner falcon	Stoop/tail-chase	Yes	Lure flying	Good
True eagles/Accipiters	Direct flying attack	Yes	Ground lure	Good
Small eagle/ Buteo/Buzzard	Direct flying attack	Yes	Ground lure	Good
Harris hawk	Direct flying attack	Yes	Ground lure	Good
Vultures	Soar/land	Yes	Ground lure	Good
Sea eagles	Glide attack	Yes	Pond/fish	Good
Barn owl	Glide attack	Yes	Ground lure	Poor
Eagle owl	Glide attack	Yes	Ground lure	Poor
Small owl	Glide attack	Yes	Ground lure	Poor

Table 6.7.2 Demonstrable search strategies

Species	Soaring	Hovering	Listening	Still-hunting	Quartering
Peregrine	Yes	No	No	Yes	No
Black falcon	Yes	No	No	Yes	Yes
Brown falcon	Yes	No	No	Yes	No
Kestrel	No	Yes	No	No	No
Little falcon	Yes	No	No	Yes	No
Black kite	Yes	No	No	No	Yes
Whistling kite	Yes	No	No	No	No
Barn owl	No	No	Yes	Yes	No
Barking owl	No	No	Yes	Yes	No
Powerful owl	No	No	No	Yes	No
Harrier	Yes		Yes	Yes	Yes
True eagles/Sea eagles	Yes			Yes	
Vultures	Yes				
Buzzards/Buteos	Yes			Yes	

Table 6.10.3 Species suitable for demonstrations.

Species	Scientific name	Average weight		Demonstrated behavior
		Male	Female	
Peregrine falcon	*Falco peregrinus*	685	900	Stooping/tail chasing
Gyr falcon	*F. rusticolus*	900	2000	Stooping/tail chasing
Prairie falcon	*F. mexicanus*	750	850	Stooping/tail chasing
Aplomado falcon	*F. femoralis*	260	400	Stooping/tail chasing
Lanner falcon	*F. biarmicus*	500	750	As above
Brown falcon	*F. berigora*	450	800	Chasing ground lure/locating food by sound
Black falcon	*F. subniger*	550	850	Stooping/tail chasing
New Zealand falcon	*F. novaezeelandiae*	300	475	As above
Saker falcon	*F. cherug*	750	1300	As above
Barbary falcon	*F. pelegrinoides*	600	750	As above
Australian kestrel	*F. cenchroides*	120	175	Hovering
European kestrel	*F. tinnunculus*	150	270	Hovering
American kestrel	*F. sparverius*	120	160	Hovering
Golden eagle	*Aquila chrysaetos*	3500	5000	Chasing ground lure
Tawny eagle	*A. rapax*	2100	3100	Soaring/chasing ground lure
Steppe eagle	*A. nipalensis*	2300	4100	Chasing ground lure
Wedge tailed eagle	*A. audax*	2100	5000	Soaring/chasing ground lure
Imperial eagle	*A. heliaca*	2000	3900	As above
Bonelli's eagle	*Hieraaetus fasciatus*	980	1900	As above
African hawk eagle	*H. spilogaster*	900	1400	As above
Little eagle	*H. morphnoides*	700	1100	As above
Booted eagle	*H. pennatus*	650	950	As above
Long crested eagle	*Lophaetus occipitalis*	1000	1400	Chasing ground lure
Wahlbergs eagle	*A. wahlbergi*	800	1400	As above
Stellar's sea eagle	*Haliaeetus pelagicus*	4000	7000	Fishing
White breasted sea eagle	*H. leucogaster*	2900	3800	Fishing
White tailed sea eagle	*H. albicilla*	3900	4800	Fishing
African fish eagle	*H. vocifer*	2000	3600	Fishing
Bald eagle	*Haliaeetus leucogaster*	3500	5000	Fishing/chasing ground lure
Red tailed hawk	*Buteo jamaicensis*	950	1100	Chasing ground lure
Red shouldered hawk	*B. linaetus*	1100	1300	As above/taking food in the air
Rough legged hawk	*B. lagopus*	750	980	As above

Table 6.10.3 Species suitable for demonstrations *continued*

Species	Scientific name	Average weight		Demonstrated behavior
		Male	Female	
Ferruginous hawk	*B. regalis*	1000	1300	Chasing ground lure
Swainson's hawk	*B. swainsoni*	700	1300	Chasing ground lure
Harris's hawk	*Parabuteo unicinctus*	650	1200	Chasing ground lure/taking food in the air
Augur buzzard	*B. augur*	1200	2100	Taking food in the air
Jackal buzzard	*B. rufofucus*	1300	2900	Taking food in the air
Common buzzard	*B. buteo*	950	2000	Taking food in the air
Broad-winged hawk	*B. platypterus*	350	450	Chasing ground lure/scavenging
Mississippi kite	*Ictinia mississippiensis*	250	320	Soaring/taking food in the air
Swallow tailed kite	*Elanoides forficatus*	400	450	As above
White tailed kite	*Elanus leucurus*	200	300	Hovering
Black shouldered kite	*E. caeruleus*	200	300	Hovering
Turkey vulture	*Cathartes aura*	2000	2500	Scavenging/locating food by scent
King vulture	*Sarcorhamphus papa*	3000*		As above
Egyptian vulture	*Neophron percnopterus*	1550	2200*	Breaking eggs with a rock
Lappet faced vulture	*Torgos tracheliotus*	5900	7900*	Scavenging
White backed vulture	*Gyps africanus*	4400	6000*	As above
White headed vulture	*Trigonoceps occipitalis*	3300	5300*	As above
Hooded vulture	*Necrosyrtes monachus*	1800	2600*	As above
Cape vulture	*G. coprotheres*	7300	10900*	As above
Eurasian griffon	*G. fulvus*	6800	8200*	As above
Andean condor	*Vultur gryphus*	9000*		As above
Barn owl	*Tyto alba*	400	500	Locating food by hearing
Great horned owl	*Bubo virginianus*	1300	1700	As above
Screech owl	*Otus asio*	160	200	As above
Barred owl	*Strix varia*	600	780	As above
Spotted owl	*Strix occidentalis*	-	-	As above
Snowy owl	*Nyctea scandiaca*	1200	1900	Glide attack/locating food by sound
Giant eagle owl	*Bubo lacteus*	680	3015	Glide attack
Spotted eagle owl	*Bubo africanus*	487	995	Glide attack
White faced owl	*Otis leucotis*	192	206	Glide attack

Chapter Seven
The Raptor Aviary

7.1 Managing the aviary display

Raptors in aviaries are forced to lead a sedentary life. They are totally reliant upon their keeper for their daily food, water, and general needs. The standard raptor aviary can be rather boring. Unlike many other species of birds, the captive raptor, be it a kestrel or an eagle, does little other than perch and stare into the middle distance. The owls are a typical example; since most of their activities are nocturnal, the general public rarely sees them doing anything. There is very little that one can do to inspire or promote activity. Thus, the daily management of a standard raptor aviary is a simple affair. It is illegal to give live food, other than fish or invertebrates, to predators, and this restriction poses a problem of behavioral and environmental enrichment. The problem of inactivity is exacerbated when crippled birds are involved. The one-winged eagle in an aviary can do little except perch, and perhaps inspire a bit of sympathy from the onlooker.

7.2 Designing the aviary

Shelter from the elements is the first requirement. The raptor must be able to retreat into shade or shelter from rain or wind. The aviary must be secure and safe from potential dangers, such as foxes and other mammalian predators. One must take into account the prevailing wind when placing the aviary, and plant vegetation to provide areas of seclusion and to act as a wind break.

Water is also vital. Bath pans or troughs should be deep enough to allow the bird to wade in up to its chest. Low perches near the water are an asset, allowing the bird to sun itself after a good bath. However, care must be taken to avoid placing the bath pans near or underneath perches or feed ledges, for obvious reasons. Public viewing areas and graphics must also be considered; the raptor's sense of security should not be compromised by allowing public access to become an intrusion. A

Figure 7.2 A simple aviary.

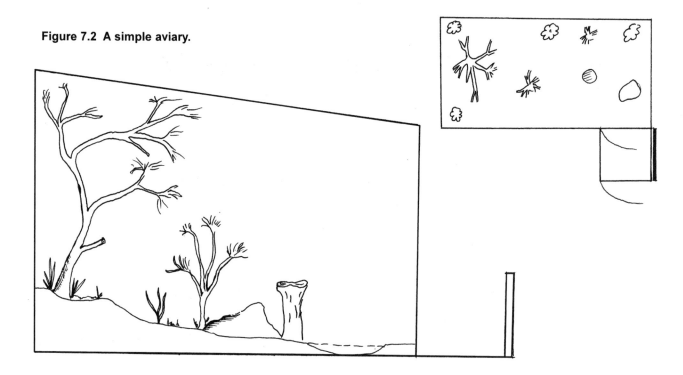

happy medium can be achieved, and thoughtful perch placement will encourage the raptor to perch in an area where it is visible but high enough above the people to feel secure.

Aviary size is comparatively important, and the general rule is "the bigger the better." Eagles that can fly require an aviary of least 80 ft. (25 m) in length and at least 16 ft. (5 m) in height (see chapter 2.2), with perches at varying heights, and placed in such a way as to allow a clear flight path from perch to perch.

Many organizations try to create an aviary that is naturalistic, but in the case of raptors, this is in reality more for the public's benefit. An aviary that is cluttered with dense vegetation and logs only reduces the amount of usable space. The sensible approach is to design the aviary for the species rather than for the public. Having a good knowledge of the raptor's behavior in the wild will be of great assistance when designing the enclosure.

7.3 PERCHING

Like the wild raptor, the captive raptor in an aviary spends a great portion of its time perching. Even those species that are naturally quite aerial are forced to be sedentary under most captive conditions. In the wild, a raptor can choose where to perch, it can find the ideal roosting site, and it can change its position to obtain shelter from wind or rain. In an aviary, the raptor has to use what has been provided. Therefore, a wide selection of comfortable perches should be offered, some in open positions and others in sheltered areas. Most birds feel more secure if they are up high, particu-

Figure 7.3a *(above)* **Passage sparrowhawk on preferred round branch on bow perch.**
Photo: Nick Fox from Understanding the Bird of Prey

Figure 7.3b *(left)* **Falcons prefer to sit on flat surfaces.** *Photo: David Hancock*

larly at night, so it is important to provide a number of comfortable, high perches, as the raptor will invariably use these more often than the lower ones. Higher perches will make the task of quick capture almost impossible, and require that the birds are conditioned to pick up food from a box in which they can be captured when necessary.

Covering weathered wood perches with astroturf or strips of coco-fiber matting will reduce the risk of bumblefoot (see Chapter 8, Veterinary aspects). Perches that are used as a feed area must be cleaned at least once a week, particularly if astroturf is being used, and the turf changed at least once every two months. The astroturf tends to flatten with continuous use, and will eventually become useless. Wide topped logs are also ideal, and these must also be cleaned on a regular basis. At the very minimum, all food scraps should be removed.

7.4 FEEDING RAPTORS IN AVIARIES

Many organizations opt for the easiest and cheapest food available. Day-old chickens regularly appear on the raptor menu, often day after day, for breeding birds and non-breeding birds alike. Even though raptors fed this diet will reproduce, day-old chickens do not constitute an adequate diet for continuous use. Many of the raptors I have seen that have been fed exclusively on this diet are not healthy looking individuals!

Mixing foods is always a good idea, as long

as the keeper remembers to consider the species with which he is dealing. Wedge-tailed eagles will eat almost anything, as will brown falcons. Kestrels can not break into thick-skinned laboratory rats and, in my experience, generally do not like rabbit. Sparrowhawks need high energy food. Mice are a good all around food for raptors, but if one is catering to dozens of captive raptors ranging from eagles to sparrowhawks, a sufficient supply of mice can become very expensive.

The captive, aviary-housed raptor has restricted flight space, and can not hunt or defend a territory, or even interact with the outside world. For these reasons, food becomes the center of their universe. Because they look forward to being fed, feeding time is the ideal time to offer some stimulation. Bones are an excellent treat for eagles, as they can spend at least an hour gleaning off the meat. This ripping and tearing also aids in keeping the bird's beak trim, and to some extent, it serves to allay boredom. Falcons can be offered chicken wings or heads for the same purpose. The quantity that each bird requires can be determined from its body weight (see Tables 9.1.1 and 9.1.2). Wild, flying raptors expend more energy than sedentary, aviary-housed birds. Over-feeding raptors in confinement can result in fat, over-weight, and generally very unhealthy birds.

The reverse of this situation is represented by those aviary-housed raptors which are uninterested in food. I have seen such birds look at their food with a total lack of enthusiasm and pick at it disdainfully before dropping it again. The healthy, well-managed bird should immediately eat what has been offered and then wipe its beak, preen, and relax. The food should be the highlight of the bird's day, not an unwanted intrusion into time that could otherwise be spent staring into the distance.

7.5 MIXING SPECIES

The habitat aviary is supposed to meet some of the specific requirements of certain species. While it is often safe and worthwhile to house various species of passerines together in the same aviary, the same is not necessarily true in regard to raptors. Careful thought must go into housing several species of raptor together. In very large enclosures, it is possible to house two or three small raptorial species, e.g., kestrels, sparrowhawks, and perhaps the Pacific baza. Eagles should always be housed alone. Many of the owls do not do well with other birds, as they are often harassed and could potentially be eaten by, or eat, their co-habitants. Peregrines kill goshawks in the wild, and goshawks kill peregrines. Eagles eat almost anything. There is also the danger of territorial aggression if pairs of birds are housed in multi-species exhibits. Successfully breeding any species in a mixed species aviary will be exceedingly difficult, if not impossible. The aviary display is best designed for single species. If a multiple species aviary is planned, several feeding stations must be established.

Being rewarded for a job well done.

Photo: Peter Karston

Malaysian eagleowl learning from experience.

Photo: David Hancock

Harris's hawk. *Photo: M. Kettle*

Author getting owl ready for release.

Photo: Richard Naisbitt

Picking up a raptor from the lure.

Photo: Richard Naisbitt

Never too young to learn.

Photo: Richard Naisbitt

A proud Wedge Tailed Eagle and handler.

Photo: Richard Naisbitt

Flight Training & Educational Programs

Andean condor flying above the crowd.

Vertical flight exercise.
Photo: Richard Naisbitt

African fish eagle getting some practice. *Photo: M. Kettle*

Kite flight training.
Photo: Richard Naisbitt

Egyptian vulture approaches emu egg to demonstrate breaking eggshell to get at yolk or young. *Photo: Richard Naisbitt*

Bird shows are popular all over the world- Jurong Bird Park.

Photo: David Hancock

Peregrine on creance. *Photo: Richard Naisbitt*

Taking off from the fist. *Photo: Richard Naisbitt*

Falcon is wearing two transmitters. *Photo: Richard Naisbitt*

Gyrfalcon-block perches are safest set on a flat surface.

Throwing lure to a falcon.
Photo: Richard Naisbitt

Bells for helping locate a bird.
Photo: David Hancock

Peregrine with leash extender.
Photo: Richard Naisbitt

Hawks / Falcons on kill

These two falcons flew as a cast and were released together.

Harris hawk on a rabbit.   *Photo: Niall Benvie*

Harris Hawk fighting a pheasant.
Photo: Niall Benvie

Tame hacked peregrine.

Male and female juevenille peregrine
on a kill.

Harris hawks flying in a cast.

Preparing for release

Peregrine preparing for release.

Flight trainging on peregrine.

Banded peregrine due for release.

Hawk eagle on a travelling perch.

Raptors and Telemetry

Satellite transmitter on a ferruginous hawk. *Photo: M. Standfield*

Ferruginous hawk with straps to attach transmitter. *Photo: M. Standfield*

An early version of a transmitter weighing over 100 grams!
Photo: Richard Naisbitt

Ferruginous hawk showing leg bell and transmitter. *Photo: M. Stanfield*

Tail with transmitter.
Photo: Richard Naisbitt

Tail mounted transmitter.
Photo: Richard Naisbitt

Note telemetry on the tail.

Juvenile female brown goshawk showing damaged tail.

Bald eagle wing showing feather growth.
Photo: David Hancock

Peregrine showing moult patterns.

David Hancock imping in coloured feathers to id in the field.   *Photo:David Hancock*

Damage feather pinched off during growth.   *Photo: Richard Naisbitt*

Imping feather, stage 2.
Photo: Richard Naisbitt

Imping feather stage 3.
Photo: Richard Naisbitt

Imping feather stage one.
Photo: Richard Naisbitt

Hooded Birds on Blocks

Hooding a harris hawk. stage 1.
Photo: Niall Benvie

Hooding a harris hawk. stage 2.
Photo: Niall Benvie

Hooding a harris hawk. stage 3.
Photo: Niall Benvie

Indian hood.
Photo: Richard Naisbitt

White goshawk-hoods can be very fancy.
Photo: Richard Naisbitt

Dutch falcon hood.
Photo: Richard Naisbitt

Arab hood.
Photo: Richard Naisbitt

Hooded peregrine on block perch.
Photo: Niall Benvie

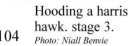

Artificial nest box for barn owls.
Photo:OWL

Harpy eagle at nest.

Raptor at nest site.

Bald eagle nesting on tower at
Boundry Bay, BC, Canada.
Photo: David Hancock

A rare occurence-3 young bald eagles at nest.
Photo: Conrad Musekamp

Steppe eagle surveying its
surroundings.
Photo: Vladimir B. Masterov

Owls do not make their own nest, but
utilize those of hawks, eagles, ravens, etc.

Golden eagle nesting on a cliff.
Photo: Peter Karston

Weathering Areas

harris hawk enjoying the morning air.
Photo: Niall Benvie

Disney weathering area. *Photo: M. Standfield*

Protected weathering area. *Photo: Richard Naisbitt*

Falcon holding and breeding
room. *Photo: Richard Naisbitt*

Outside weathering area. *Photo: M. Standfield*

106

Osprey foot, this perch is too smooth, but note the toe size.
Photo: Richard Naisbitt

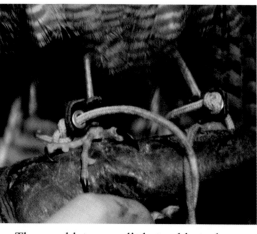

These anklets are a little too big and heavy, they may cause leg problems.
Photo: Richard Naisbitt

Perches such as these have to potential for leashes to get entangled.
Photo: M. Standfield

Correct way of holding an eagle

Red tailed hawk- wrapping rope over the perch is a good way to prevent foot problems.
Photo: David Hancock

This block is too small.
Photo: Richard Naisbitt

Note the astro turf makes the top of the block soft. *Photo: Niall Benvie*

Natural and cheap perches.

Perches

Morning preen on block perch.
Photo: Joe Roy III

Travelling box.
Photo: Niall Benvie

Red tailed hawk- note rope wrapped around perch.
Photo: David Hancock

Shelf perch close-up.
Photo: Richard Naisbitt

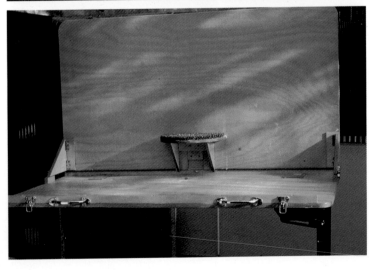

Collapseable shelf and perch table.
Photo: Richard Naisbitt

A very ornate perch with barred windows.

Falcon under exam, note talk guard.
Photo: Richard Naisbitt

Taking a blood sample from black kite, via sugular vein.
Photo: Richard Naisbitt

Black kite under aneasthesia.
Photo: Richard Naisbitt

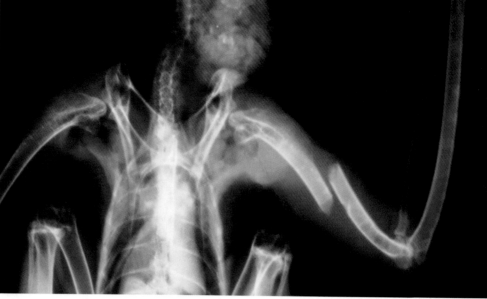

Fractured humerus.
Photo: Richard Naisbitt

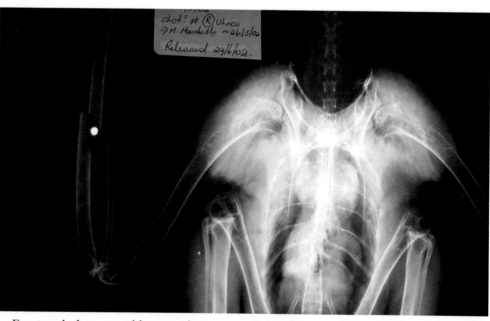

Fractured ulna caused by gun shot. note pellet at fracture site.
Photo: Richard Naisbitt

Old fractured humerus in swamp harrier. *Photo: Michelle Manhal*

Old fractured humerus in swamp harrier.
Photo: Michelle Manhal

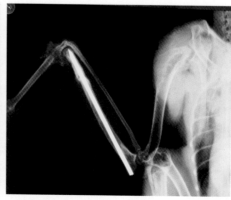

Ulna splint *Photo: Richard Naisbitt*

Weighing Birds

Weighing and recording room.   *Photo: David Hancock*

Training goshawk to sit on the scale.
Photo: David Hancock

Weight recordal is vital part of raptor husbandry.
Photo: Niall Benvie

Eagle chick being weighed at the orphaned wildlife rehabilitation center.
Photo: OWL Delta, BC, Canada

Chicks are often weighed daily to monitor growth rate, especially in the rarer species such as this andean condor chick.
Photo: Richard Naisbitt

Mexico City Zoo raptor aviary.
Photo: David Hancock

Mexico City Zoo raptor aviary.   *Photo: David Hancock*

This pen is too narrow for a large bird of prey.   *Photo: Richard Naisbitt*

Andean condor avairy,
Taronga Zoo Australia.
Photo: Eric Edwards

King vulture aviary.

Photo: David Hancock

Miscellaneous Raptors

Broad-winged Hawk

Long-eared Owl

Snowy owl

Crested Caracara

Some of the
marvelous raptors
from
Encylcopedia of
Aviculture.

Secretary Bird

Bateleur eagle

Coopers Hawk

Peregrine Falcon

Cape Griffon

CHAPTER EIGHT
RAPTOR MEDICINE

8.1 INTRODUCTION

This chapter is not intended to be a comprehensive review of raptor diseases and management (for which the reader is referred to Fowler 1986). Rather, it discusses the conditions met with frequently by the author during the management and treatment of wild raptors presented for rehabilitation.

To survive successfully in the wild, a bird of prey must be in excellent physical condition and able to fly almost perfectly. Without this ability, it will be unable to compete successfully with those birds which can perform at maximum efficiency, and, as a result, it will slowly starve to death or be predated by others. Because of these exacting demands, many birds are euthanized after their initial clinical examination.

8.2 INITIAL FIRST AID

A bird of prey that can be picked up or handled is injured, unless it is a tame or hand-reared individual. Any attempt to restrain the bird will produce an escape response. The injury that prevents this escape may be subtle and difficult to detect. For this reason, all injured raptors must be taken to a veterinarian for evaluation.

Because the majority of raptors presented to rehabilitation centers are suffering from trauma, they are often in shock. This can be treated, as in mammals, using intravenous (IV), intraosseous (IO), or subcutaneous (SC) fluids. Birds suffering the effects of shock are often dehydrated. Dehydration in birds can be assessed, as in mammals, by pinching the skin, particularly over the tarsometatarsus. Although bird skin is less elastic than mammalian skin, in a well hydrated bird, once the skin is released it should return to its normal position. If dehydrated, the skin will remain in the pinched position (Redig 1993a).

First, the normal weight of the bird needs to be known. For these calculations, a female peregrine falcon will be used as an example. The bird should weigh approximately 900 grams. If it is 10% dehydrated, it will need 90 ml Lactated Ringers. Maintenance requirement is 50 ml/kg/day, which, for this bird, amounts to 45 ml. In the first 24 hours, the bird needs to receive its basic maintenance requirement plus half the deficit, i.e., 45 + 45 = 90 ml. This is divided into four. Therefore, the bird receives 22.5 ml IV four times during the first day of treatment.

The same process is repeated on the second day, taking into account that the deficit has been reduced through the first day's treatment. Thus, the bird is given maintenance plus half the remaining deficit, i.e. 45 + 22.5 = 67.5 ml. This is divided into three equal doses of 22.5 ml..

On the third day, the remaining fluid is administered, i.e. 45 + 22.5 = 67.5 ml. Again, this is divided into three doses of 22.5 ml per dose.

Finally, on the fourth day, the maintenance dose alone is provided in two equal IV doses of 22.5 ml each.

An alternative method of calculation is to administer 2% of the bird's body weight in fluids IV to the bird four times on the first day. Using the same 900 g peregrine as an example, 2% of 900 g equals 18 ml. Administered four times during the day, this totals 72 ml on Day 1. On Days 2 and 3, this is given three times for a total of 54 ml per day, and on Day 4 twice, for a total of 36 ml. This results in a total of 216 ml over the four days, as opposed to 270 ml by the previously described method. As all calculations are approximate, the 2% guide can be used to simplify matters.

If the bird is not obviously dehydrated, but in shock, an initial intravenous bolus of Lactated Ringer's solution should be administered in a single 20 ml/kg dose and the clinical response of the bird monitored.

The use of corticosteroids is controversial, but dexamethasone can be given at 5 mg/kg IV if the bird is presented within 48 hours of the injury occurring. Beyond this time, corticosteroids are unlikely to have any significant effect.

Subcutaneous fluid administration is less effective in birds than mammals, as their skin is poorly vascularized. However, if IV or IO access is not possible, the regime described above can be administered SC.

Head trauma is common, and is treated with corticosteroids, fluids, and maintenance in a quiet, dark, cool area. If the prognosis is favorable, these birds will start to show improvement within 48 hours of presentation.

8.3 ANAESTHESIA

Isoflurane is the agent of choice for both induction and maintenance. Most birds can be maintained on 2% Isoflurane. Larger species, such as eagles, may need higher levels for maintenance, i.e., 3% or more. Intubation is simple, as the glottis lies at the base of the tongue and can be easily visualized.

Monitoring is the same as for mammals, using heart rate, respiratory rate, and reflexes. In birds, assess righting reflex, lack of tone in the beak, and withdrawal reflex.

The respiratory system is extremely efficient in birds. A network of air sacs functions as a series of bellows to pump air through the lungs during both inspiration and expiration. The lungs expand minimally. This produces an unidirectional flow of air, as opposed to the in and out movement occurring in mammals. The avian air capillaries are much smaller than mammalian alveoli, the blood-gas barrier is thinner, and pulmonary blood flow is higher. Consequently, birds can absorb approximately 20% more oxygen from the air than mammals can. A diaphragm is absent. Because of their superior gas exchange capability, birds can rapidly change planes of anesthesia. This can result in a sudden, explosive arousal from anesthesia. It can also result in unexpected cardiac arrest. With halothane anesthesia, respiratory and cardiac arrest occur almost simultaneously. Isoflurane is safer, as there is a lag period between respiratory and cardiac arrest. A recent study examining isoflurane use in bald eagles found that 75% of birds developed cardiac arrhythmias at some stage during anesthesia (Aguilar et al. 1995). However, hypothermia, hypercapnia, and ECG abnormalities were more marked in galahs *Eolophus roseicapillus* anaesthetized with halothane than with isolflurane (Jaensch et al. 1999). If respiratory arrest occurs, the anaesthetic should be turned off and the patient ventilated, with special care being taken not to overinflate and rupture air sacs. Cardiac arrest is almost always irreversible.

With a high metabolic rate, birds lose heat quickly. Therefore, a heating pad should always be used, although a recent study found that radiant heat was superior to a warm-water blanket for maintaining core body temperature (Phalen et al. 1996). As few feathers as possible should be plucked, and alcohol used sparingly, if at all, as a skin disinfectant.

Procedures involving anaesthetized birds must be performed as efficiently as possible, with no waste of time. The risk of anaesthetic death increases dramatically with time.

Accessible blood vessels
1) Jugular vein. This vein runs in a featherless tract along the side of the neck. The right jugular is easier to visualize and sample.

2) Brachial vein. This vein is found on the medial aspect of the wing, running over the elbow. The accessibility of this vein is good in large birds, but it is very fragile and will readily form a haematoma. Digital pressure should be applied following venipuncture. This vein is not suitable for postoperative catheters.

Figure 8.3a Brachial vein.

3) Medial metatarsal vein. Located on the medial aspect of the tarsometatarsus, this vein does not form a haematoma. It cannot be accessed in brown goshawks, as it is covered by an impenetrable keratin scale in this species.

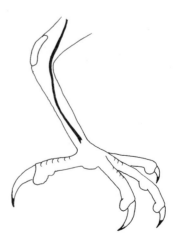

Figure 8.3b Medial metatarsal vein.

4) Intraosseous. A spinal needle can be introduced into the distal extremity of the ulna using sterile technique (Ritchie et al. 1990). This can be connected to a catheter, and fluids administered. Absorption of fluids is almost as rapid from this site as it is if administered intravenously. Birds tend to be intolerant of intravenous catheters postoperatively, but intraosseous catheters can be easily taped in place and are generally well tolerated.

8.4 MANAGEMENT OF SOFT TISSUE INJURIES

Most wild raptors are presented with injuries rather than disease. These are commonly the result of collisions with cars, fences, or other objects, or gunshot wounds. Whether it be a laceration or a puncture, all the standard principles of wound treatment apply.

The bird should be anaesthetized to decrease stress and struggling. Bird skin is very thin and has a relatively poor blood supply. Wounds tend to develop plugs of necrotic tissue and coagulated blood, which delay healing. These need to be removed and fresh, healthy tissue exposed.

The wound is then explored to determine its extent and severity. Necrotic tissue is debrided and the wound flushed with a solution of chlorhexidine or normal saline. Iodine solutions exacerbate tissue necrosis and delay wound healing (Swaim and Lee 1987).

Following thorough cleaning, the wound should be sutured, if possible. A study in rock doves *Columbia livia* found that polydioxanone (PDS) was the best suture material to use, as it caused minimal tissue reaction and was absorbed slowly (Bennett et al. 1997).

Polyglactin 910 (Vicryl) produced the most intense tissue reaction, but was the most rapidly absorbed. Chromic catgut also caused an intense inflammatory reaction, but was absorbed slowly. Its use was not recommended. Nylon and stainless steel caused minimal tissue reaction but tended to cause haematomas and seromas.

If suturing is not possible, the wound can be allowed to heal by secondary intention. Ointments such as live yeast cell derivative (Preparation H, Whitehall Laboratories) can be used to stimulate healing (Swaim and Lee 1987; Liptak 1997). Care must be taken with ointments to avoid smearing too much on the feathers.

During the initial stages of injury, a wet-to-dry adherent dressing is used to remove necrotic debris. Once the reparative stage is reached, this is replaced with a non-adherent dressing (Liptak 1997). Sticky tape, Elastoplast, masking tape, and other sticky bandages should never be used, as they damage the feathers and leave a residue. A self adherent material such as Vetrap is required.

8.5 MANAGEMENT OF ORTHOPAEDIC INJURIES

These are the most common injuries sustained by raptors, representing 33.8% and 50% of all cases presented in two separate studies (Fix and Barrows 1990; Morishita et al. 1998). Careful evaluation is required to determine if the fracture is likely to be amenable to treatment.

8.5.1 Birds which should be euthanized are those which have:

a) a compound fracture, i.e., a piece of bone has pierced the skin and is obviously visible. If these are fresh and not severely contaminated, treatment can be attempted using lavage and systemic antibiotics. However, severely contaminated fractures have a poor prognosis for recovery and generally progress to osteomyelitis despite treatment.

   Avian heterophils lack some of the enzymes found in mammalian neutrophils. Consequently, they form caseous rather than liquid pus. This impedes drainage, hinders penetration of antibiotics, and makes it difficult to remove all infected material. Repeated vigorous lavage with normal saline or chlorhexidine is required, but this will also delay wound healing.

b) fractures near or involving a joint, and dislocations. The elbow is the most commonly luxated joint. For elbow luxations, it is not sufficient simply to bandage the wing. Contraction of tendons and arthritis will result. The luxation must be reduced and the bones held in their anatomical position, either by bandaging or using external fixation devices. Joint imbrication can be attempted to stabilize the joint. Many birds, however, will develop arthritis and will not fly well enough for release. In two reviews, four out of eight cases and three out of twelve cases were released following surgical attempts at reduction (Martin et al. 1993; Ackermann & Redig 1997).

c) one or both eyes missing or severely damaged. Eye loss means the bird can no longer judge distances adequately, and will therefore be unable to hunt successfully.

d) loss of the use of a leg. Birds with one leg cannot hunt effectively and are prone to developing bumblefoot due to the uneven weight distribution.

e) digit two and the hallux (rear digit) missing on one or both feet, or the hallux alone missing on both feet. Without these digits, the bird will be unable to kill its prey.

Although birds may be found surviving in the wild with the above-mentioned injuries, these are the exception rather than the rule. The most important thing is to produce a bird that has the best possible chance of survival after release.

8.5.2 Management of specific injuries

As stated previously, raptors need to be in virtually perfect condition to survive in the wild. They are much like elite human athletes. Many fractures can be repaired, but not well enough for release. As with human athletes returning from injury, they may appear to function perfectly well at rest or with light exercise, but, when forced to work hard, deficits in maneuverability or endurance may appear. These deficits, although they may seem relatively minor, will compromise the bird's ability to catch fit, uninjured prey on a regular basis. Often a deficit such as this may not appear until long after the initial surgery, when the bird is being exercised prior to release. If a fracture is treated immediately and heals with no complications, the bird is still likely to require at least three months in captivity before being ready for release.

Because of the demands placed on wild birds, it must be realized that the success rate of raptor orthopedics is relatively low. Studies report a 30–40% release rate for birds admitted for treatment (Wisecarver and Bogue 1974; Snelling 1975; Duke et al. 1981; Fix and Barrows 1990; Naisbitt 1998).

To an inexperienced practitioner, being presented with an injured raptor may appear quite daunting. At first glance, the bird has little in common with the more familiar dog or cat. However, it is important to bear in mind that the similarities are greater than the differences. All that is really required is an ability to work from first principles and a desire to experience and learn from new challenges.

When first examining the potential orthopedic case, one must bear in mind that few injuries are symmetrical. While experience is an obvious advantage, inexperience need not necessarily be a major handicap. Palpate both wings (or legs). If something feels amiss in one wing, feel the other wing for comparison. If both wings feel identical, it is likely that the perceived anomaly is normal. However, if the wings are not identical, then there is likely to be a problem.

The same is true for radiology. If unsure of a possible fracture or dislocation, compare both sides of the radiograph. In order to be able to do this, symmetry is very important. If the bird is in a twisted position, it will be difficult to compare the two sides.

Historically, bandaging wings has been a popular way of dealing with fractures in raptors. Advantages of this include a minimal investment of time and effort coupled with the fact that the procedure is relatively inexpensive and non-invasive. However, success has not been good in returning birds to flight using this method of treatment.

The greatest problem with the commonly used figure of eight bandage is that the bandage impinges on the bird's propatagium (Brown and Klemm 1990). This soft tissue structure lies anterior to the humerus, elbow, and radius/ulna, linking the shoulder to the carpus. The leading edge of the propatagium contains the very elastic ligamentum propatagiale and its associated blood supply.

Prolonged bandaging in this area results in fibrosis of the ligament and possible compromise of the blood supply with avascular necrosis of the propatagium. If the ligament fibroses, then the wing cannot reach full extension and the bird will be unreleasable. Disuse osteoporosis has also been recorded in pigeons, bone loss occurring at a rate of 2.96% per week of the wing being bandaged (Wimsatt et al. 1998).

Some success has been achieved in reversing the wing contraction by using ultrasound. However, ultrasound did not affect the bone loss (Wimsatt et al. 1998). In most orthopedic cases bandaging is not required, or desirable, if internal fixation is used. If bandaging is to be used, it should not remain in place longer than a week without some form of physiotherapy occurring to keep the wing supple and its range of extension normal.

Many of the following orthopedic techniques are based on Redig (2000). An excellent review of avian orthopedic anatomy has been produced by Orosz et al. (1992).

Surgical preparation is as for mammals. All feathers around the surgical site must be removed. They should be pulled firmly but gently in the same direction as the feather. Care should be taken not to twist the feather or damage the follicle, as this will result in abnormal feather regrowth or no regrowth at all.

Feather removal is a painful process for the bird, and response to this procedure is a good indication of the level of anesthesia.

Skin preparation is as for mammals. Birds are as susceptible to infection as mammals, and all the same aseptic techniques need to be adhered to.

Raptors are checked under anesthesia one week after surgery to ensure that no problems have occurred. If all is well, the bird is again checked three weeks after surgery, and a radiograph taken. Depending on radiological evidence of healing and fracture stability, the pins may be removed or more time may be required. Following pin removal, a further seven days elapse before any flight training should be attempted.

Spine

Birds with spinal fractures are alert, but incapable of flight and unable to stand. Because birds have a spine that is quite rigid, vertebral displacement is often minimal, limiting the usefulness of radiographs in detecting a fracture. The most common site for fractures to occur is anterior to the synsacrum. The main differential diagnosis is organophosphate poisoning (see 8.11). If the spine is not fractured but bruising has occurred in the surrounding soft tissue, improvement should occur with cage rest and dexamethasone given at 2–5 mg/kg intramuscularly. However, if the spine is fractured and the spinal cord damaged, euthanasia is the only option.

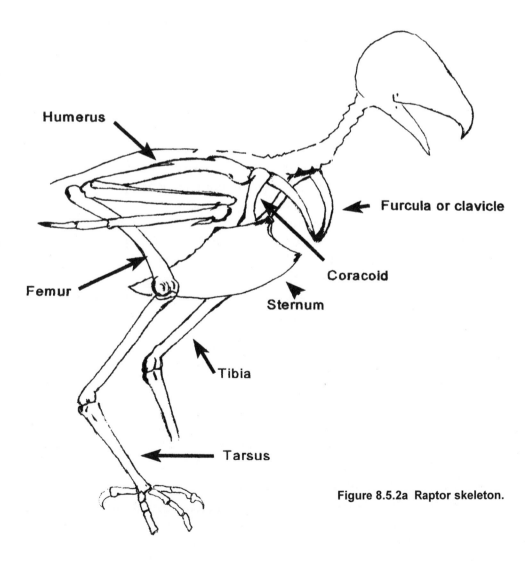

Figure 8.5.2a Raptor skeleton.

Coracoid

The coracoid is a large bone that extends from the shoulder to the sternum. It is the strut which supports the pectoral muscles. Birds frequently fracture the coracoid by colliding with blunt objects such as cars or windows.

Typically the bird is presented with a normal stance. The wings do not droop, but when stimulated, the bird cannot rise more than 3 ft. (1 m) off the ground. Palpation may reveal some crepitus in the shoulder, or abnormal wing extension, but this is not reliable. Accurate diagnosis requires a radiograph.

For the radiograph to be effective, the bird needs to lie symmetrically in dorsal recumbency. A good radiograph will have the sternum superimposed over the spine. If the bird is twisted, diagnosis will be difficult due to rotation and superimposition of the bones on one another.

Typically, the coracoid is fractured midshaft. Success has been achieved by cage resting small birds such as wrens and finches. However, surgical intervention is required for heavier birds with high wing-loadings, such as peregrine falcons.

The surgical approach involves incising along the sternum and the clavicle and reflecting the pectoral muscles. Hemorrhage is not as great as might be expected. When the muscles are reflected, a small keyhole aperture is visible. The fracture ends can be visualized in this area. Manipulation is difficult due to the restricted space. A prominent vascular/nerve plexus, which must be avoided, is also present in the vicinity.

An intramedullary pin is inserted in the distal fragment to emerge at the shoulder. It is then retrograded into the proximal fragment. Care is required to ensure the pin does not enter the thoracic cavity. If this occurs, a rush of air can be heard and anaesthetic gas can be detected. If the pin is retrograded slightly out of the thorax, there should be no complications. Unlike mammals, which require a completely sealed thoracic cavity, this is not necessary for birds.

The surgical site is closed routinely, reattaching muscles to the bone and closing the skin. Healing takes approximately four weeks, after which the pin is removed.

Clavicle

The clavicle is infrequently fractured. Management is by cage rest. Alternatively, holes can be drilled through the fracture ends and the fragments wired together.

Scapula

The scapula is also infrequently damaged. Treatment involves cage rest.

Humerus

When the humerus fractures, the surrounding muscles contract to stabilize the fracture site and decrease pain. This results in overriding of the fragments. If the wing is bandaged, the fracture may heal, but the wing will be shortened and the bird will not be able to be released. Surgical intervention is essential to produce a bird fit for release.

The best technique involves a combination of intramedullary pinning and external fixation. The bird is placed in ventral recumbency and the humerus approached dorsally. The IM pin is inserted on the dorsal aspect, just cranial to the distal humeral condyles, and driven cranially through the distal humeral fragment into the proximal fragment.

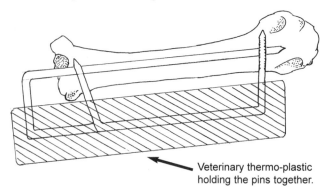

Veterinary thermo-plastic holding the pins together.

Figure 8.5.2b External fixature on a fractured humerus.

If it is not possible to align the fracture non-surgically, then an incision must also be made directly over the fracture site and the fragments physically aligned while the pin is driven through. The pin should not exit at the shoulder. Pliers are then used to bend the protruding caudal segment of pin dorsally and then cranially so that it lies parallel to the humerus. The pin has, in effect, formed a U shape.

Next, two fixator pins are placed into the humerus at right angles to the bone. The cranial pin is placed through the shaft of the humerus and not through the deltoid crest.

The caudal pin is inserted through the distal condyles.

Pins should engage both cortices but not emerge on the bone's medial aspect.

Prior to fixator placement, the wing should be placed in a normal physiological resting position to ensure no rotation occurs and the wing rests in normal alignment.

Following insertion, the cranial fixator pin is bent caudally, parallel to the length of the humerus, and the caudal pin is bent cranially. The two fixator pins and the IM pin should all be lying parallel to each other outside the humerus. A piece of thermoplastic splint material (Orfit Vet, Orfit Industries, Wijnegem, Belgium) is then heated until it is malleable and folded over the three exposed pins. This will cool and harden, resulting in a very rigid framework that provides rotational stability and maintains the length of the bone.

An alternative approach is to keep all three exposed pins perpendicular to the long axis of the humerus. A length of penrose drain is inserted over the pins and filled with a cement such as methyl methacrylate. When this hardens, it forms a similarly sturdy frame. Bandaging is not required.

Radius/ulna

Bandaging has often been recommended for fractures of these bones. However, this often results in a poor union or the development of synostoses where the radius and ulna fuse together. This compromises the bird's ability to rotate the wing, severely hampering its ability to turn and maneuver.

The radius is a very mobile bone and should always be repaired surgically, even if the ulna is intact, to prevent delayed and non-unions. If the radius is intact, the ulna does not need to be repaired surgically unless there is great displacement of the fragments. The wing can be bandaged in a figure of eight wrap using Vetrap, bearing in mind the caveats mentioned above. The bandage needs to be changed at least weekly, and passive physiotherapy must be used to keep the wing's motion within the normal range.

The ulna is repaired by inserting a pin through the caudal aspect of the bone, near the elbow, and driving it through the proximal fragment into the distal section. Care must be taken to avoid penetrating the joint and damaging the carpus.

The radius can be pinned in a retrograde fashion with the pin exiting at the carpus. Given the position of the radius, this should cause minimal damage to the joint.

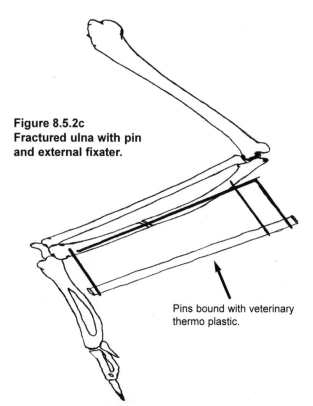

Figure 8.5.2c
Fractured ulna with pin and external fixater.

Pins bound with veterinary thermo plastic.

Metacarpus

Metacarpal fractures are difficult to manage due to a lack of soft tissue and fragile blood supply. The bone is approached ventrally to avoid damaging the feathers, which insert directly on the bone dorsally (Orosz 1994). An intramedullary pin is introduced directly into the distal fragment and then normograded into the proximal fragment.

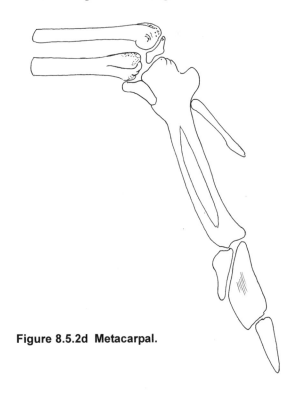

Figure 8.5.2d Metacarpal.

Femur

The femur is similar to the humerus, as it is surrounded by strong muscles which cause overriding of the fracture fragments. Surgically, the bone is approached on the lateral aspect. A pin is introduced at the fracture site into the proximal fragment. Due to the anatomy of the femur, the pin can exit from the bone proximally without compromising the hip joint. The pin is then retrograded into the distal fragment.

This can be used as the sole method of repair, but a more sturdy repair that will elim-

inate rotation involves external fixation, similar to that described for the humerus. The distal fixator pin is driven through the condyles and the proximal pin is seated just distal to the greater trochanter. All three pins are then bent so that they lie parallel to the long axis of the femur, and they are fixed in place with thermoplastic splint material or a penrose/methyl methacrylate combination.

Due to the femur's close proximity to the body, bandaging is not possible and will not provide adequate fracture fixation.

Tibiotarsus

The tibiotarsus is approached medially. Several techniques have been described (Meijetal 1996). An intramedullary pin is introduced into the proximal fragment, exiting at the stifle. This is then retrograded into the distal fragment. With this method, rotation of the leg is possible.

An alternative approach is to use external fixation. Two pins are introduced perpendicular to the bone into the proximal fracture fragment, and two are introduced into the distal fragment. The pins are passed through the bone and are bent parallel to it medially and

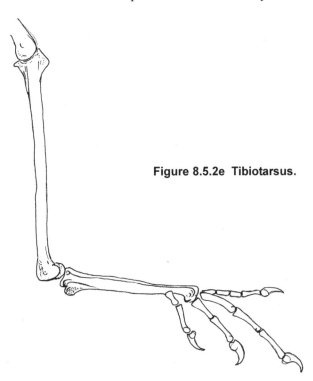

Figure 8.5.2e Tibiotarsus.

laterally. They are then linked together with thermoplastic splint material for stability.

For maximum stability, a combination of intramedullary pinning and external fixation can be used.

Tarsometatarsus

This bone has no true marrow cavity (Hess 1994) and is not suitable for intramedullary pinning. External fixation, similar to that described for the tibiotarsus, is the method of choice.

Phalanges

These can be splinted using a ball bandage. A ball of gauze is created to approximate the size of the foot. This is then bandaged to the plantar aspect of the foot with the phalanges wrapped around the ball in a physiological position.

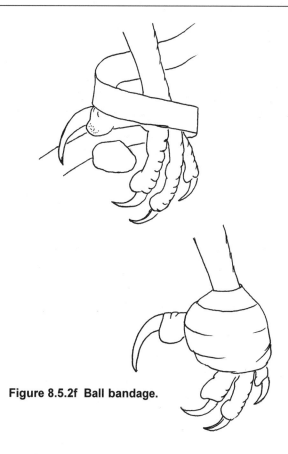

Figure 8.5.2f Ball bandage.

8.6 OCULAR TRAUMA

A large number of injured raptors have eye injuries. A survey at the Avian Clinic in Cornell revealed a percentage of 14–28% (Murphy 1987). Although some of these have obvious corneal or anterior chamber injuries, many also have posterior chamber or retinal damage, which cannot be detected without a thorough ocular examination. This is complicated by the fact that birds have striated muscle in the iris, which does not respond to topical atropine. Success at dilating the pupil has been achieved by injecting 0.01–0.03 ml 3% D-tubocurarine directly into the anterior chamber. The resulting mydriasis lasts up to 18 hours. However, this method carries the risk of introducing infection and possibly damaging intraocular structures. An alternative is to administer 0.2 mg/kg vecuronium systemical-

ly. This induces mydriasis after approximately 26 seconds, which lasts for about 26 minutes. Repeated topical administration of muscle relaxants results in only partial mydriasis due to poor drug penetration across the cornea (Korbel 2000). It is important to keep the bird out of direct sunlight during the period of mydriasis.

Vision may be difficult to assess, as birds inconsistently exhibit a menace response, and will have a normal pupillary light reflex unless retinal damage is severe (Davidson 1997). Owls, in particular, may exhibit anisocoria. This is normal, unless one eye remains consistently dilated. Birds with unilateral blindness may present with a head tilt in an attempt to compensate for the loss of vision in one eye (Murphy 1987).

Birds with corneal injuries may exhibit blepharospasm and a serous ocular discharge. Fluorescein can be used to stain any corneal ulcers. These can be treated with topical antibiotic drops or ointments. Drops should be administered six times per day, and ointment, three times per day. Due to the stress involved in catching a wild bird this frequently, it may be better to perform a temporary tarsorrhaphy. This can be checked at weekly intervals to monitor the healing progress.

Hyphaema is a common finding. If not severe, it will resolve spontaneously over several days (Davidson 1997). If severe, scarring of the iris may result.

It has been reported that 31% of traumatized birds have severe posterior chamber lesions (Korbel 2000), often the result of bleeding from the pecten, a darkly pigmented pleated structure attached to the retina protruding into the vitreous. It is generally regarded as providing nutrients to the avascular retina (Murphy 1987). Severe hemorrhage will lead to blindness in that eye. Mild hemorrhage will respond to dexamethasone 2–3 mg/kg injected intramuscularly. Recovery can take a month or more.

In assessing a bird with eye lesions for release, its history must be taken into account. Depending upon why the bird was presented, an individual in good body condition with an old eye injury has likely been surviving well in the wild. However, a thin bird with a relatively recent injury may not be coping and needs to be carefully assessed.

If there is any doubt, the bird should be flown, and its ability to maneuver and negotiate obstacles determined.

8.7 BUMBLEFOOT

Bumblefoot, or infectious pododermatitis, is a condition of the feet, usually caused by trauma. In addition to raptors, it is commonly seen in heavy birds such as swans and pelicans, as well as in waterfowl forced to spend a lot of time on their feet. The main predisposing factor is incorrect perching. The rehabilitator should never place birds on concrete, as this will abrade their feet. Perches that are uniform or smooth will inevitably lead to bumblefoot. Perches that are too small will result in talons piercing the foot and causing infection.

Staphylococcus is the most common causative agent. This organism is not part of the normal flora of raptors (Needham 1981); in the Spanish imperial eagle, its appearance has been shown to be associated with handling by humans. This study recommends using gloves whenever handling these birds to decrease the transmission of this organism (Ferrer and Hiraldo 1995).

Severe, untreated bumblefoot can result in osteomyelitis of the foot and, via bacterial emboli, endocarditis of the heart valves. A number of treatment strategies have been published (Riddle 1981; Redig 1993b; Remple 1993; Degernes 1994).

The plantar aspect of the normal raptor foot contains numerous papillae. In the first stage of bumblefoot, the foot appears reddened and these papillae are reduced in size. The skin may also appear quite thin. At this stage the condition will respond to a change in substrate to a more suitable perch.

If untreated, the skin will wear through and ulcerate, exposing the underlying soft tissue. From here, caseous material will accumulate in the foot and necrosis of the tendons will follow. If still unattended, osteomyelitis will result and infection will track along the tendon sheaths. At this stage, prognosis is extremely poor and euthanasia the likely outcome.

When the bird is initially presented with bumblefoot, it should be anaesthetized for its initial examination. A scab will be present on the plantar surface of the foot. This should be removed or soaked off using dilute chlorhexidine. Once the scab has been removed, the foot cavity is flushed with chlorhexidine or saline. The object is to remove as much necrotic material and caseous pus as possible.

Once this is done, a wet-to-dry bandage is applied by using sterile gauze soaked in chlorhexidine. This is held in place by using a ball bandage to contain the foot. To make a ball bandage, gauze is rolled into a ball. The size of the ball depends on the size of the foot. The toes should be able to reach around the ball in a normal position. This bandage is then strapped to the foot using Vetrap. Initially, the bird is anaesthetized and the bandage changed on a daily basis until no obvious caseous or necrotic material is visible. At this point, the foot cavity can be fully or partially sutured. Success has been achieved with the use of framycetin impregnated beads (Leukase Kegel, Merck, Vienna, Austria) instilled into the foot. These are left in the foot to dissolve with time (Walzer, pers. comm.).

Alternatively, polymethylmethacrylate beads impregnated with antibiotic can be used (Remple and Forbes 2000). To make these beads, five parts polymethylmethacrylate is mixed with one part piperacillin and rifampicin or pefloxacin and rifampicin. This can be sterilized and formed into beads which can be placed into the affected foot for seven to ten days.

As well as local treatment, systemic antibiotics are required. Rifampicin has good activity against *Staphyllococci*, and penetrates granulomas well, but resistance occurs rapidly if used on its own (Remple and Forbes 2000). Amoxycillin/Clavulanic acid combinations at 85 mg/kg twice a day or enrofloxacin 15 mg/kg twice a day can also be used. These should be given intramuscularly initially, followed by orally, to decrease the stress associated with frequent handling.

Time to resolution can be prolonged, up to several months. An added complication is, if the bird has unilateral bumblefoot, it will put more weight on the unaffected foot. This will lead to trauma and possibly bumblefoot in this foot also. To prevent this, the bird should be placed on soft material, such as a foam pad, or the other foot can be padded with an interdigitating bandage during the convalescent period. However, all this effort and treatment will be wasted unless the predisposing factors are identified and addressed.

8.8 TRICHOMONIASIS

This disease is also termed canker or frounce. It is caused by a small, motile, flagellated protozoan. Although it can occur in any raptor species it is most commonly observed in goshawks due to their pigeon eating tendencies. Pigeons are the main carrier of the organism.

The most common symptom is caseous, or cheesy-looking, material in the oral cavity. This is found adjacent to the tongue, on the floor of the oral cavity, and in the pharynx. In very severe cases, necrosis and caseous material has been found in the crop. The material is adherent to the mucosa and, if physically removed, will result in mucosal bleeding.

A wet preparation of the material can be

examined under the microscope. This must be fresh, as the examination is searching for motility. Once the organisms have died they can be extremely hard to find. In most cases of trichomoniasis, it is unusual to find motile organisms and treatment has been based on the presence of caseous lesions alone.

It is important to bear in mind that caseous lesions will also occur with candidiasis, capillariasis, vitamin A deficiency, and pox infection. However, these are less common.

Treatment is generally easy and effective.

The caseous material is debulked and the bird is treated with carnidazole (Spartrix 10 mg/tablet, Boehringer Ingelheim Pty. Ltd., Artarmon, NSW, Australia), which is a treatment for pigeons, at 20 mg/kg orally, once. Usually, all lesions disappear within a couple of days. If not, the dose can be repeated.

The organism is susceptible to dessication and cold. Freezing pigeon carcasses for at least 24 hours prior to feeding will destroy it (Bailey et al. 2000).

8.9 ENDOPARASITISM

All wild birds of prey will be carrying a variable endoparasite burden. A routine fecal examination will reveal the presence of strongyle, capillarid, ascarid, cestode, and other parasite eggs.

Wild birds can be treated with ivermectin 0.2 mg/kg subcutaneously, pyrantel 50 mg/kg orally, praziquantel 10 mg/kg orally, or fenbendazole 20 mg/kg orally once a day for seven days.

Serratospiculum is a common parasite of peregrine falcons, usually found at necropsy in the air sacs. The female produces a larvated egg which passes up the respiratory tract to the throat, where it is swallowed. The eggs then appear in the feces. Grasshoppers and locusts are used as intermediate hosts (Anderson 1972). Levamisole, at 10 mg/kg, and ivermectin have been used with some success against this parasite (Smith 1993).

8.10 ECTOPARASITISM

Most raptors carry lice and hippoboscid flies. All bird lice are biting lice which are species specific. When present in large numbers, they can cause irritation and feather damage due to excessive preening and scratching. They can be treated with insecticide powders suitable for puppies or kittens, usually containing carbaryl or pyrethrin. Ivermectin is also effective.

Hippoboscid flies, or flat flies, are related to the sheep ked. They can transmit blood parasites such as Haemoproteus (Peirce 1981), but are otherwise insignificant. Flat flies often leave the bird during examination, landing on the human handler. Apart from their presence causing annoyance, they are inoffensive; they do not bite or transfer zoonotic diseases.

8.11 POISONING

8.11.1 Lead

Raptors which have been poisoned by lead are frequently reported in North America and South Africa. While poisonings are less commonly reported in Australia, they certainly do occur, with lead poisoning being the most prevalent.

A bird that has been shot and has lead pellets in its wings, legs, or chest will not develop lead poisoning. The impact of the pellets may cause significant damage, but once lodged in the tissues, the pellets themselves cause minimal problems unless they are interfering mechanically with a nerve or blood vessel. In most cases, removing pellets causes more problems than leaving them in.

Poisoning occurs when birds ingest lead. This is most commonly observed in birds that feed on carcasses of animals shot by hunters. Feeding captive birds on animals that have been shot with a shotgun is a good way to cause lead poisoning. Only animals killed with a single shot should be used as feed.

Symptoms of lead poisoning include anemia, weight loss, diarrhea, depression, and neurological signs such as nystagmus, head tremors, seizures, and blindness. Histologically myocardial necrosis, fibrinoid necrosis of blood vessels, and renal tubular necrosis with or without inclusion bodies my be apparent. Blood levels over 0.2 ppm indicate exposure to lead. Birds with levels above 0.6 ppm show mild clinical signs, and those with levels above 1.0 ppm will show severe symptoms (Redig 1993a).

Treatments consists of 50 mg/kg calcium ethaminediaminetetracetic acid (EDTA) administered twice daily intramuscularly. This is given for four days on, two days off, four days on, two days off, for four treatment periods, as it is potentially nephrotoxic (Redig 1993a).

Treated birds generally improve quite dramatically with the first 24 hours. Alternatively, D- penicillamine can be given orally at 55 mg/kg twice a day (LaBonde 1991). Greater success has been reported combining the above two drugs (Dumonceaux and Harrison 1994). Both CaEDTA and penicillamine are used until the bird is asymptomatic. Penicillamine alone is then used for a further 3–6 weeks.

8.11.2 Organophosphates

Organophosphates function by inhibiting acetylcholinesterase. This prolongs the effect of acetylcholine at neurotransmitter sites, leading to continued stimulation, followed by fatigue and death from respiratory failure. Raptors are generally affected by consuming poisoned birds.

Clinical signs include ataxia, a spastic nictitans, a detached attitude, and inability to fly with no signs of trauma. Occasional convulsions, characterized by rigid paralysis, clenched talons, opisthotonos, and rapid respiration can occur. Birds are generally in good condition. Post mortem lesions are minimal, pulmonary edema often being the only abnormality.

Diagnosis can be made by measuring serum cholinesterase levels. Unfortunately, normal values are not known for most species. One study indicated that levels below 0.9 International Units per milliliter were abnormal (Porter 1993). If the bird is dead, diagnosis can be made by measuring brain cholinesterase. In one study, normal levels ranged from 14–27 cholinesterase activity units in diurnal birds of prey, and 16–20 units in owls (Hill 1988). A 20% depression is indicative of exposure, while a 50% depression is diagnostic.

Due to the difficulty in obtaining normal cholinesterase levels, two studies have compared the ratio of brain cholinesterase to the number of muscarinic cholinergic receptors across a number of species. Ratios less than 0.345–0.5 were strongly suggestive of intoxication (Prijono and Leighton 1991; Burn and Leighton 1996).

Alternatively, stomach contents and liver can be submitted frozen for organophosphate analysis.

Treatment consists of 0.5 mg/kg atropine administered intramuscularly. If no improvement has occurred within 15 minutes, the diagnosis should be reviewed (Porter 1993).

8.11.3 Organochlorines

Poisoning by these compounds is not as prevalent as it has been in the past. These chemicals persist for extended periods in the environment and accumulate in the fat. As long as they stay in the fat there are usually no problems. However, if the bird is nutritionally stressed and needs to mobilize its fat reserves, clinical signs will occur. These include ataxia, blindness, convulsions, and emaciation.

No lesions are present at post mortem. For diagnosis, brain and liver should be wrapped in aluminum foil, frozen, and submitted for organochlorine analysis. Plastic containers should not be used, as some plastics contain organochlorine residues. Recorded lethal levels in the brain exceed 20 ppm DDT, 5 ppm chlordane, 0.8 ppm endrin, 3 ppm dieldrin (Porter 1993), 8 ppm heptachlor, and 200 ppm mirex (Wiemeyer 1996).

There is no antidote for organochlorine intoxication and treatment is symptomatic.

8.12 MISCELLANEOUS CONDITIONS

The above injuries and diseases represent the most frequently encountered conditions when dealing with raptors being rehabilitated for release. This section will touch briefly on other conditions which may be encountered.

8.12.1 Aspergillosis

Aspergillosis is a fungal infection of the air sacs and lungs. The fungus itself is ubiquitous in the environment and causes secondary infections in stressed, debilitated birds, particularly in moist, humid environments.

Species predilections have been reported, with penguins being particularly susceptible. Among the raptors, gyrfalcons, golden eagles, red-tailed hawks, and rough-legged hawks have been reported to be especially sensitive (Redig 1993c).

Prevention centers around minimizing stress and ensuring good ventilation. Avoid the use of any type of moldy material. Prophylaxis with itraconazole (Sporanox 10 mg/ml, Janssen Pharmaceutical, Titusville, New Jersey, USA) at 10 mg/kg once a day orally has been used with some success.

Treatment is difficult and generally not successful. Drugs used include amphotericin B (Fungizone 50 mg/vial, Bristol-Myers Squibb Pharmaceuticals Pty. Ltd., Noble Park, Victoria, Australia) nebulized for twenty minutes at a dose of 7.5 mg/bird. Alternatively, itraconazole at 10 mg/kg twice a day orally has also been used. A newer human antifungal agent, terbinafine (Lamisil 250 mg/tablet, Sandoz Australia, North Ryde, New South Wales, Australia) has shown promise when administered at a dose of 10 mg/kg once a day. When used in combination it may also enhance the efficacy of amphotericin B and itraconazole.

8.12.2 Candidiasis

Candidiasis is caused by a yeast infection in the oral cavity. It presents similarly to trichomoniasis with caseous material in the oral cavity. If a smear is made of this material and stained with Diff Quik, numerous small blue oval bodies can be seen. Budding will also be apparent. Treatment involves oral nystatin (Nilstat 100,000 IU/ml, Wyeth Australia, Baulkham Hills, New South Wales, Australia) given at 100,000 IU/kg three times a day. To be effective, the drug must contact the organisms. Therefore, it should be administered directly into the mouth, and not by crop tube.

8.12.3 Capillariasis

Capillariasis can also mimic trichomoniasis. A smear of the lesion will reveal oval shaped *Capillaria* eggs with bipolar plugs. Treatments is as described in 8.9.

8.12.4 Pox

Pox is caused by a virus. Lesions usually appear on unfeathered parts of the legs and head, but can also occur in the oral cavity. Generally, lesions begin as papules, vesicles, or pustules which progress to form scabs. The eyelids are a particularly favored site (Samour and Cooper 1993). Treatment is symptomatic, aimed at removing scabs, keeping eyes clean, and hand or force feeding the bird if the oral cavity is affected.

8.12.5 Herpesvirus

Controversy exists over the use of pigeons as food for raptors. Pigeons carry a herpesvirus which may spill over into raptors. Herpesvirus disease has been recorded in peregrine falcons, common kestrels, merlins, red-necked falcons, prairie falcons, and American kestrels (Gerlach 1994). Clinical signs include depression, weakness, anorexia, and death. Lesions include multifocal necrosis, particularly in the liver, spleen, pancreas, lungs, and kidneys. Despite the practice of regularly feeding frozen pigeons to the raptors at Healesville Sanctuary, this condition has not been recognized.

8.13 RELEASE CONSIDERATIONS

By now, much time and effort has been invested in the raptor. It has survived starvation, dehydration, soft tissue injuries, fractured bones, ocular lesions, and bumblefoot. It has been nursed back to health and is now ready reconditioning and training as described in the earlier chapters, prior to release.

If a bird is concussed and only spends a few days in captivity, its fitness is unlikely to be compromised and it can be released from an aviary with no training. However, after two to three weeks in treatment, fitness levels will have declined markedly and the bird must be exercised prior to release. Releasing birds from an aviary with inadequate conditioning training is inhumane and cannot be condoned. The need for conditioning and training cannot be overly stressed. Some people in the rehabilitation movement resist the necessary falconry techniques of conditioning and rely on merely chasing a bird around the aviary, totally misunderstanding the need of increasing motivation and hunting skills that are so essential for survival in the wild.

SUMMARY

The rehabilitation and release of raptors is potentially very rewarding, as long as it is understood that many injured birds will be unsuitable for release and euthanasia may be the kindest option. Some birds not fit for possible release might serve other educational, display, or captive breeding programs.

It is imperative that adequate follow up is available to monitor birds that are released. Unfortunately, few raptor releases in the past have included follow up studies (Wisecarver and Bogue 1974; Snelling 1975). Long term survival has been estimated through the use of band returns, (Servheen and English 1979; Duke et al. 1981; Ingram 1988; Sweeney et al. 1997; Martell et al. 2000) or by radio tracking individual birds (Hamilton et al. 1988; Martell et al. 1991). Follow up information is vital to assess success and modify techniques if they need refining. Any release guidelines should be viewed as being very dynamic. Nothing is cast in stone, and all guidelines should be continually scrutinized and allowed to evolve to provide the best possible care for the bird.

The importance of adequate flight training and exercise cannot be over-emphasized. We want to give each bird the best possible chance of survival once it is returned to the wild. Life in the wild is not a form of idyllic Utopia, as is sometimes depicted. It is extremely demanding, and only the best and fittest will make it through. This is as it should be.

By placing continual demands on individuals and species as a whole, evolution continues to function, ensuring the long term health and stability of the ecosystem. By returning unfit birds to that ecosystem we are causing the death of that individual.

Many of the birds rehabilitated represent common species. The rehabilitation of these birds provides little conservation value. However, it does result in a greater understanding of the species involved, its requirements, its strengths and weaknesses, and a development of techniques which can be used in the future, should other species become endangered or vulnerable in the wild.

It also brings us closer to realizing how little we still know about the workings of the ecosystem, how interdependent the many parts are, and how any tinkering must be done intelligently, treading lightly and acting conservatively. So many of the ramifications of our actions are unknown until later. The intelligent watchmaker keeps all the parts until he comprehends their workings and is wise enough to understand that the whole is much greater than the sum of the parts.

CHAPTER NINE
THE RAPTOR DIET

9.1 DIETARY REQUIREMENTS

Proper diet is one of the more important components of rehabilitation and general captive raptor management. Wild raptors have a high attrition rate, with many birds starving to death before completing their first year. This is due to a combination of factors, including insufficient food and lack of foraging experience. The amount of

food a raptor needs for basic body maintenance is inversely proportional to body weight; a small raptor weighing less than 400 grams will need at least 10–20% of its body weight on a daily basis, while an eagle weighing 5000 grams will need only 5% of its body weight.

The immediate response of many rehabilitators and falconers, when confronted with a

Table 9.1.1 Food consumption of raptors. (Richard Naisbitt)

Species	Weight range Male / Female	Min (g)	%body weight	Max (g)	% body weight
Peregrine falcon	685 / 900	68/ 90	10	102 / 135	15
Saker falcon	750 / 1300	75/ 130	10	112 / 195	15
Gyr falcon	900 / 2000	90 / 200	10	135 / 300	15
Lanner falcon	500 / 750	50 / 75	10	75 / 112	15
Prairie falcon	750 / 850	75 / 85	10	112 / 127	15
Barbary falcon	600 / 750	60 / 75	10	90 / 112	15
Aplomado falcon	260 / 400	26 / 40	10	39 / 60	15
New Zealand falcon	300 / 475	30 / 47	10	45 / 71	15
European kestrel	150 / 270	30 / 54	20	37 / 67	15
Australian kestrel	120 / 175	24 / 35	20	30 / 43	15
American kestrel	120 / 160	24 / 32	20	30 / 40	15
Brown falcon	450 / 800	45 / 80	10	67 / 120	15
Black falcon	550 / 850	55 / 85	10	82 / 127	15

Species	Weight range Male / Female	Min (g)	% body weight	Max (g)	% body weight
Little falcon	220 / 310	22 / 31	10	33 / 46	15
Golden eagle	3500 / 5000	305 / 500	10	525 / 750	15
Wedge tailed eagle	2100 / 5000	210 / 500	10	315 / 750	15
Tawny eagle	2100 / 3100	210 / 310	10	315 / 465	15
Steppe eagle	2300 / 4100	230 / 410	10	345 / 615	15
Imperial eagle	2000 / 3900	200 / 390	10	300 / 585	15
Bonelli's eagle	980 / 1900	98 / 190	10	147 / 285	15
African hawk eagle	900 / 1400	90 / 140	10	135 / 210	15
Little eagle	700 / 1100	70 / 110	10	105 / 126	15
Booted eagle	650 / 950	65 / 95	10	97 / 142	15
Long crested eagle	1000 / 1400	100 / 140	10	150 / 210	15
Wahlbergs eagle	800 / 1400	80 / 140	10	120 / 210	15
Stellar's sea eagle	4000 / 7000	200 / 350	5	40 / 700	10
White breasted sea eagle	2900 / 3800	290 / 380	10	435 / 570	15
White tailed sea eagle	3900 / 4800	390 / 480	10	585 / 720	15
African fish eagle	2000 / 3600	200 / 360	10	300 / 540	15
Bald eagle	3500 / 5000	350 / 500	10	525 / 750	15
Red tailed hawk	950 / 1100	95 / 110	10	114 / 132	12
Red shouldered hawk	555 / 630	55 / 63	10	83 / 94	15
Rough legged hawk	750 /1045	75 / 98	10	112 / 156	15
Ferruginous hawk	1000 / 1300	100 / 130	10	150 / 195	15
Swainson's hawk	700 / 1300	70 / 130	10	105 / 195	15
Harris's hawk	650 / 1200	65 / 120	10	97 / 180	15
Augur buzzard	1200 / 2100	120 / 210	10	180 / 315	15
Jackal buzzard	1300 / 2900	130 / 290	10	195 / 435	15
Common buzzard	950 / 2000	95 / 200	10	142 / 3000	15
Broad winged hawk	350 / 450	35 / 45	10	52 / 67	15
Mississippi kite	250 / 320	25 / 32	10	37 / 48	15
Swallow tailed kite	400 / 450	40 / 45	10	60 / 67	15
White tailed kite	200 / 300	20 / 30	10	30 / 45	15
Black shouldered kite	200 / 300	20 / 30	10	30 / 45	15
Turkey vulture	2000 / 2500	200 / 250	10	300 / 375	15
King vulture	3000*	300	10	450	15
Egyptian vulture	1550 / 2200	155 / 220	10	232 / 330	15
Lappet faced vulture	5900 / 7900	590 / 790	10	885 / 1185	15
White backed vulture	4400 / 6000	440 / 600	10	660 / 900	15

starving raptor, is to feed it. If the rehabilitator is absolutely certain of the species and the sex, than he should be able to ascertain the bird's condition. One should not try to force-feed a malnourished raptor a crop full of meat, bones, and fur. It will be unable to digest these items, leading to decomposition of the food in the crop, followed by ingluvitis and possible septicemia. The bird must be started back onto solids gradually (Redig 1993a).

Upon initial presentation, the starving bird is administered 20 ml/kg Lactated Ringer's solution diluted 50:50 with 5% dextrose IV. This is done three times a day for three days.

Oral feeding can commence with the second fluid treatment. An oral supplement such as Nutripet (Troy Laboratories Pty Ltd, Smithfield, NSW, Australia) can be used. If a 900 gram female peregrine falcon is used as an example, its basal metabolic rate (BMR = $4.125 \times K$, which is 78 for non-passerines, x weight in kilograms$^{-0.25}$) should be approximately $4.125 \times 78 \times 0.9^{-0.25} = 330$ kj/kg = 297 kj for the bird.

Resting metabolic rate is approximately 2.5 times this figure, or 743 kj. This is how many kilojoules the bird will require per day at rest.

Nutripet contains approximately 1500 kj/100 g. Therefore, the falcon will need approximately 50 g of Nutripet per day. This is divided into three feedings of 17 ml each. Once the bird is coping with this, it can be started on solid food. This should consist of lean meat with no casting material. One kilogram of meat should be supplemented with one tablespoon of calcium carbonate. The bird can be fed by hand, using a pair of forceps. The bird should be treated as though it were a nestling of five days old; only offer more food if the crop is empty. On no account should the crop be completely filled. The bird needs to be observed to ensure the crop is emptying regularly. If this is the case, the amount fed can be gradually increased over a week.

The bird may also benefit from 2 mg/kg dexamethasone, B complex vitamins equivalent to 10 mg/kg thiamine, and iron dextran at 10 mg/kg, all injected intramuscularly (Redig 1993a). Research has shown that dexamethasone causes a dramatic increase in blood glucose levels (Kaufman et al. 1993).

Remember there are many reasons for starvation.

1. The raptor may have an injury that prevented hunting.
2. It may be inexperienced and starving simply due to a lack of foraging proficiency.
3. It may be suffering from an infection that has prevented it from hunting efficiently.

Once a normal weight has been reached for the species and sex concerned, feeding can be confined to once per day, offering the appropriate amount per meal.

Table 9.1.2 Feeding nocturnal raptors. (Richard Naisbitt)

Species	weight range (grams)	Diet	% of body weight/day
Powerful owl	1000–2000	Rodents	5–10%
Barking owl	700–800	Rodents	5–10%
Morepork owl	230–320	Rodents	10–20%
Rufous owl	1000–1800	Rodents	5–10%*
Barn owl	350–420	Rodents	10–15%
Eastern grass-owl	350–420	Rodents	10–15%
Australian masked-owl	700–1000	Rodents	5–10%
Greater sooty-owl	340–400	Rodents	10–15%*

Table 9.1.3 Food consumption of diurnal raptors. (Richard Naisbitt)

Species	Body weight (g)	Min (g)	% body weight (g)	Max (g)	% body weight
Brown goshawk	330 (female)	30*	9	60	18
Brown goshawk	560 (female)	30*	5.3	90	16
Collared sparrowhawk	120 (male)	21*	17	41	34
Collared sparrowhawk	200 (female)	21*	10	40	20
Peregrine	520 (male)	50*	9	80	15
Peregrine	900 (female)	50*	5	110	12
Tawny eagle	3100 (female)	80*	2	200	6
Wedge-tailed eagle	4100 (female)	100*	2	300	7
Australian hobby	220 (male)	20*	9	50	22
Australian hobby	310 (female)	20*	6	70	22
Australian kestrel	130 (male)	20*	15	30	23
Australian kestrel	180 (female)	20*	11	40	22
Barking owl	680 (Female)	50*	7	80	11
Barking owl	720 (Male)	50*	6	80	11

* weight loss noticeable or significant after minimum consumption.

In some instances, it is necessary to feed the captive raptor more than the specified percentages and then work out, from what has not been eaten, the exact daily requirement.

Weather conditions should also be taken into account; during cold weather, the raptor will inevitably require more food. This is an important consideration in the colder parts of any country.

Nutrient compositions of a range of raptor foods are presented in Table 9.1.4. These figures are based on work performed by Redig (1993a), Tabaka et al. (1994), Dierenfeld et al. (1996), and Clum et al. (1996). The work by Clum et al. (1996) found that prey diet composition had little effect on body composition. They also concluded that whole domesticated prey is an inadequate source of Vitamin E, manganese, and copper. Exotic birds may require up to ten times more Vitamin E in their diet than the levels recommended for poultry (Dierenfeld and Traber 1992). Peregrine falcons fed unsupplemented quail developed symptoms of Vitamin E deficiency. These were corrected when the diet was supplemented with 220 IU of Vitamin E per kilogram of diet (Dierenfeld et al 1989).

Different food types will have different energy values. Red meats are richer in terms of the calorie content, and certain species do better than others on red meat. The small bird-eating raptors, for example, do not thrive on rabbit.

A day-old chicken weighing 41 grams has a gross energy value of about 24.83 kilojoules/gram. A mouse weighing 30 grams has an equivalent energy value of 24.67 kilojoules/gram. Pigeon meat is even richer. Day-old chickens should be used only as a supplement, not as a main diet, and certainly not for growing raptors.

Table 9.1.4 Nutrient Composition of a Range of Raptor Foods.

Item	Chick	Hamster	Pinkie Mice	Adult Mice	Pinkie Rats	Adult Rats	Quail
DM %	24.2	30.3		31.0		33.8	38.8
Energy kj/g	22.85	24.67		24.67		24.18	
Protein %	67.4	49.8		66.8		78.6	71.7
Lipid %	21.0	34.7		16.9		34.9	49.2
Ash %	5.4	7.5		12.5	8.5 7		
Ca %	2.08	2.51	1.17	1.73	1.85	3.00	2.4
P %	1.47	2.03		1.72		1.48	
Mg %	0.05	0.12	0.11	0.09	0.14	0.15	0.04
Na %	0.71	0.46					
K %	0.80	0.88					
Fe ppm	118	237	181.3	171.6	275.8	280.0	57.4
Cu ppm	7	12	19.2	7.9	60.6	15.9	1.9
Mn ppm	5	45	0.2	8.7	6.2	17.8	4.5
Zn ppm	72	94	82.5	58.0	113.6	75.5	41.4
Vit A IU/kg				1759122		49256	36883
Vit E IU/kg				88.0		73.0	100.3

Ca = Calcium. P = Phosphorus. Mg = Magnesium. Na = Sodium. K = Potassium. Fe = Iron. Cu = Copper. Mn = Manganese. Zn = Zinc.

The ideal diet for any raptor should be as close to the natural as is possible, taking into account training programs, where food intake might have to be governed or controlled. Any strenuous work loads that may be placed upon a raptor will need to be compensated by good nutrition. Quail, rodents, and pigeons are good choices. Day-old chickens are used by many organizations as a main diet, but by themselves are nutritionally inadequate and should therefore be used strictly as a supplement, not as the primary or long-term diet. Whole food should be given regularly, such as whole quail and whole rats. Excessive fat and no exercise can be dangerous. Thus, in an aviary, the raptor will sit and eat. This behavior can be attributed to a lack of motivation to do anything else. Old, spent chickens, quail, or mice are fine, but not if the bird is inactive. Remember that many breeders of chickens,

quail, or rodents are not concerned with the longevity of their product, but with fast growth rates; it is therefore hard to predict what the final product will do to the captive raptor (Clum et al. 1996).

Nutrition affects health, not only in raptors but in a myriad of organisms. The health of the captive raptor is dependent on what it is fed. The composition of the prey animals used for food may in turn be influenced by their own level of nutrition. A domesticated and humanely killed prey animal that has been poorly fed and has suffered or is deficient in certain minerals will not keep a captive hawk healthy.

The raptor has to break down the food it is fed, moving it from the crop to the stomach. Once the indigestible parts of a meal, such as fur and bones, have been separated, the bird is left with the portion of the meal that can be metabolized. The indigestible portions are formed into a bolus that is "cast" up through the beak.

The whole point of feeding a starving raptor easily digestible foods is to reduce the energy needed to break it down. The sick hawk needs a food source that will increase its weight without using energy to break it down (see start of this chapter). The healthy hawk needs a diet that will maintain it over and above the energy needed for activity. An eagle in an aviary needs enough food for basic maintenance, but the requirements for the maintenance of a hard-flying eagle in the hunting field will be higher. These requirements depend on the kind of food it is fed, the weather conditions, and above all on the exercise load placed upon the bird. With this logical approach, success can be expected.

Figure 9.1 A passage saker perched on a fine Arab block perch. The bird is also hooded to protect it from potential environmental disturbances.
Photo: From Arab Falconry *by Roger Upton*

CHAPTER TEN
EQUIPMENT

10.1 EQUIPMENT AND HARDWARE FOR HOLDING RAPTORS

For the demonstrator or rehabilitator, there is a wide selection of equipment available, ranging from hoods to the right type of perches, and then onto bells and transmitters. Every year there seems to be new companies offering new and more "efficient" equipment. Weighing devices are being constantly improved. And while some things, like hoods, fortunately never change, opinions do.

What has become very clear is the necessity of using equipment that is safe and reliable.

The old traditional jesses, with their big swivel slits, are not an option for any bird; nor are screen perches and long leashes. There are many new designs for perches, leashes, lures, and all sorts of attachments, but if one is planning to tether or hood or in anyway restrain a raptor, he should not try to save money by using a cheap option. Being practical is one thing, being stupid is another. This is good advice for the new falconer/demonstrator or the inexperienced rehabilitator.

10.2 USING HOODS

Many hood designs are a product of hybridization, Anglo/Indian, Syrian/Arab, and a whole lot more in between, but they all serve the same purpose, which is shutting out any adverse visual stimuli to reduce the occurrence of excited reactions. Training a bird to wear a hood should be carried out in conjunction with

Illustration: Elizabeth Darby

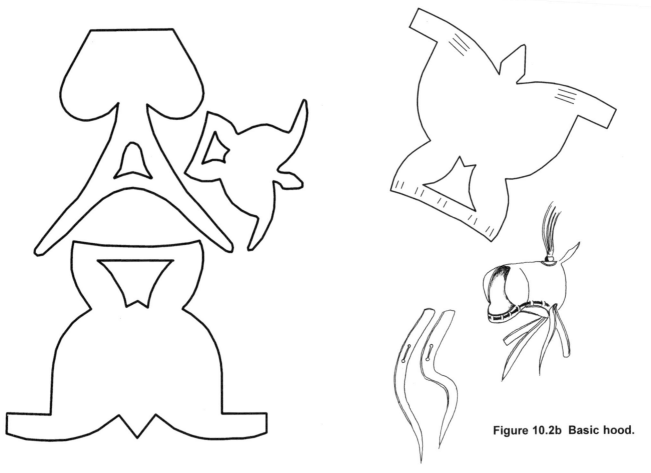

Figure 10.2a Various hood patterns.

Figure 10.2b Basic hood.

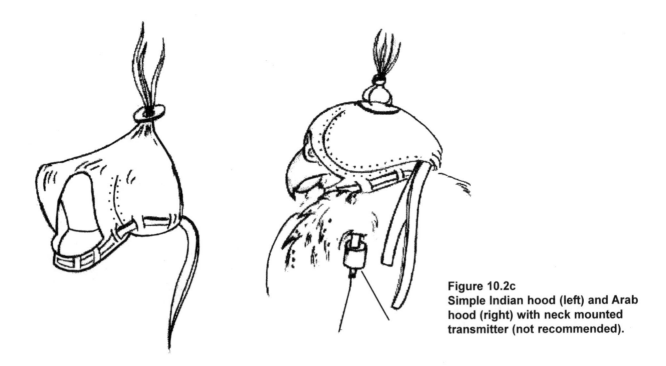

Figure 10.2c
Simple Indian hood (left) and Arab hood (right) with neck mounted transmitter (not recommended).

basic training. The hood should not be used to shut the trainer out.

The bird should become accustomed to the trainer and the hood at the same time. Gentle handling is obviously necessary, and jamming a hood onto a bird's head will not bring forth the required results, but only serve to make the bird very reluctant to wear it. Like much of the training process, hooding a raptor comes down to simple common sense. A bird's refusal to accept a hood can often be traced back to an early problem, and once this has been identified, remedial measures can be taken.

Hoods serve their purpose only if the trainer is proficient with their use. Hood-trained birds are easier to work with when replacing anklets, coping beaks, or carrying the birds for short distances through areas where they otherwise might panic. If one is inexperienced or lacks confidence with using hoods, and needs to transport a raptor, then a well-built transport box is just as useful.

If one does intend to use hoods, then it is vital to contact someone who has expertise in making and using hoods (see Further Reading). There are many hazards that can complicate the use of hoods. For instance, birds can be lost wearing hoods, or badly fitting hoods can cause eye problems. If the wrong type of hood is left on a bird overnight, it can cause choking when the raptor tries to cast. Using caution is the best advice I can offer.

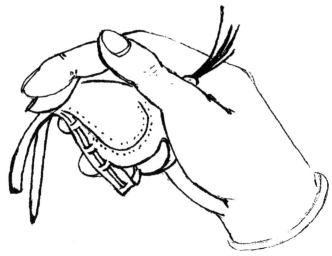

Figure 10.2e One method of holding a hood when hooding a falcon.

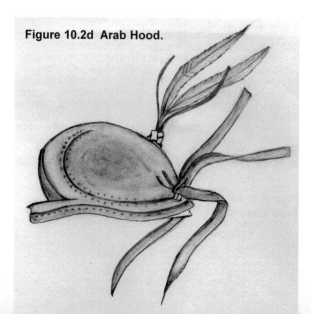

Figure 10.2d Arab Hood.

**Figure 10.2f
Hooded falcon on bow perch.**

10.3 JESSES AND LEASHES

Just as the wrong hood is dangerous, so are badly made jesses and leashes. A bird lost with a leash attached will die, and this is negligent. When flight training a rehabilitation bird, one should use the minimal amount of equipment, always avoiding trailing jesses or big swivel slits. This also applies to birds being used in a demonstration. Remember that if there is even a remote chance of something catching a trailing jess, then it will probably happen. Ideally, any bird being flown should only be wearing anklets, or possibly clip-on jesses that can be removed when the bird is exercised.

Figure 10.3a Flying with slitted jesses is dangerous.

The swivels in Figure 10.3b, are ball bearing swivels, commercially made for fishing. These are suitable for most small to medium raptors. Large eagles require something more substantial. Swivels for large birds can be purchased from falconry dealers, of which there are many addresses on the Internet. Alternatively, one might use heavy duty swivels purchased from equestrian centers. I have used these in the past. They are functional, but need to be checked on a regular basis.

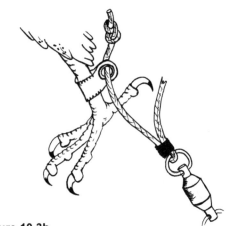

Figure 10.3b
Nylon jesses tied off with a figure of 8 knot.

With the Arab leash attachment, the jesses are similar to those found in Figure 10.3c, but have no slits for the swivel. A nylon loop is attached to the swivel and the jesses are tied onto the loop. They can be left on, or removed, when the bird is flown. Some birds will learn to untie these, so extra caution is required when using this attachment. The Arab leash attachment is not recommended for eagles, as the odd bate here and there will tighten the knot, making it almost impossible to remove.

In essence, it is wise to consider what bird one is going to fly, where it will be flown, and the number of potential obstacles that could catch a dangling or trailing jess. The bird should be observed, and the manner in which

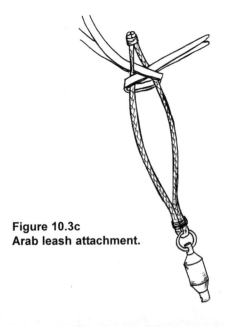

Figure 10.3c
Arab leash attachment.

it fiddles with its equipment noted. Some falcons chew at their leash, others do not. Leather leashes are good, but require constant maintenance and are not suitable for eagles. Nylon leashes, or nylon cord with a central core, are better, being superior to leather.

Most leashes are attached to a perch with the standard falconer's knot, which works well and is a traditional method of tying a bird to a perch. One can, however, use whatever knot he prefers, as long as it can be tied and untied with one hand. The knot must be infallible, and the bird must not be able to undo it. The falconers knot can be tied off first, and then another knot added above it for extra security. Leashes should always be checked on a daily basis.

Leash length is also an important factor. No more than twice the bird's body length is ideal for the distance from the perch to the bird's legs. If the leash is any longer, the sudden jerk that stops a bird when it hits the end of the leash can be damaging. Rubber dampers can be used to alleviate any sudden "stop shock," but these must be checked regularly. The dampers are often made from surgical tubing, and are attached to the perch first and then to the leash. The leash is also tied to the perch separately. When the bird bates, the tension is taken up by the rubber; if the tubing breaks, the leash is still attached and the bird is safe.

In summary, jesses, anklets, and leashes are tools used to restrain a raptor when it is on the glove or in a weathering area. Good equipment is vital, but even expensive equipment can fail, so check every part of it. There is no point in having to say in retrospect "I should have checked the leash, or if only..."; a bird that escapes with a leash on will die. If species are mixed together in a weathering yard, such as goshawks and kestrels and larger falcons, equipment breakage can be equally disastrous. If a goshawk, for example, breaks a leash or the jesses, the chances are it will kill the nearest bird. I have had a goshawk drag a heavy bow perch inch by inch until she was close enough to kill a bird twice her size. There is no excuse for this; it was complacency alone that lead to disaster.

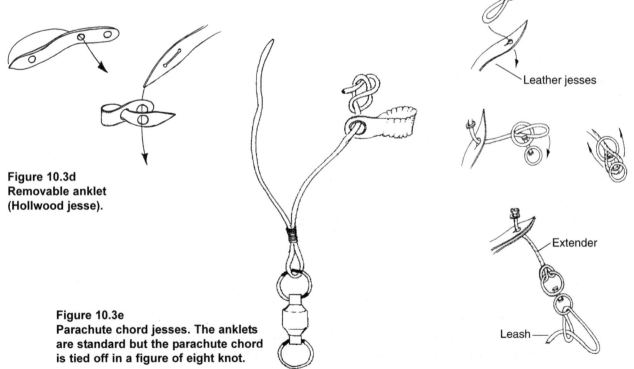

**Figure 10.3d
Removable anklet
(Hollwood jesse).**

**Figure 10.3e
Parachute chord jesses. The anklets
are standard but the parachute chord
is tied off in a figure of eight knot.**

Leather jesses

Extender

Leash

**Figure 10.3f
Parachute chord leash extender.**

10.4 SWIVELS

The standard leash attachment needs a swivel of some sort. The swivels that are found on dog leashes are not suitable, and should never be used for this purpose. In order to save time and avoid potential problems, one should contact a falconry equipment manufacturer and buy the appropriate equipment. One can make his own jesses and leashes, but not his own swivels. Large "Sampo" ball bearing swivels are good for small to medium sized raptors, such as peregrines, gyrfalcons, sakers, and prairie falcons. Small to large goshawks or sparrowhawks can be managed with the same type of swivel, but eagles need something more substantial. One must be careful about taking short cuts, avoiding clip swivels or dog spring clip swivels. These are not satisfactory for raptors. They break easily, resulting in lost birds. The best equipment is needed, whether the bird is being flown for rehabilitation, in a demonstration, or recreationally.

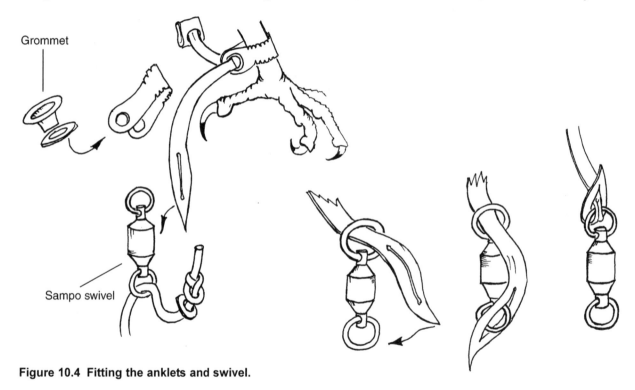

Grommet

Sampo swivel

Figure 10.4 Fitting the anklets and swivel.

10.5 MAKING LURES

The reasons for using a lure must be fully understood before it is made or used (see Chapter 6.3). In many cases, the lure does not have to resemble a real animal. Raptors can differentiate between live prey and a lure, e.g., falcons will chase a pair of dried wings. So in reality, no matter how many hours you spend painting your lure and trying to make it look authentic, the hawk knows the difference. It is, however, preferable to start with something reasonably realistic in appearance; then, as training is completed and the bird knows what the lure represents, it can be changed. This is particularly applicable to birds undergoing rehabilitation.

Lures should be made in such a way so as to ensure their longevity and ease of maintenance. Dragging a rabbit lure through the wet grass, day after day, causes a great deal of wear and tear. Having an eagle rip a lure to shreds when it is soggy will cost another few hours in making a replacement. Plain, simple leather lures that are water proof and durable are perfect.

Figure 10.5 shows a standard falcon lure for any large falcon. It is a leather pad, filled with stuffing, which can be of any material. The wings are leather and can be painted red or white, or a real pair of wings can be attached. This lure weighs about 300 grams and can be carried by most medium to large falcons, but it is soft and will not cause damage to the falcon if any impact occurs. I have made many leather lures, often painstakingly painting them to resemble a duck or a pigeon, but I still use an old leather kangaroo hide pad with two ragged wings, which is just as effective. All of my falcons come back to this, and I even use a similar lure for goshawks.

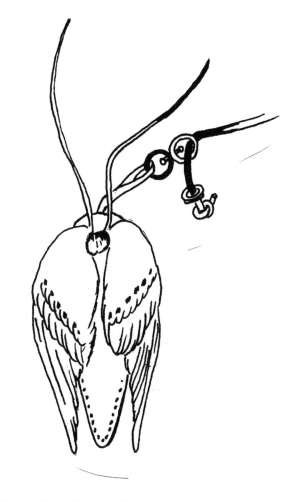

Figure 10.5 Standard falcon lure.

10.6 THE CREANCE

Before any raptor is ready for its first free flight, it must serve its apprenticeship, for want of a better word, on a training line or creance. A bird's competence in performing many of the behaviors required for its first free flight can only be assessed after a period of time, which will vary according to individual circumstances. The creance prevents a new bird from disappearing over the horizon. It is a life line that is used until the raptor is responding reliably to the lure or glove, and until it knows what is expected of it.

The creance can also be used to test fly raptors that are due to be released. This type of flight assessment is used widely, particularly in the United States. Braided or woven nylon line about 2.5–5 millimeters in diameter, with a test weight of around 120 lb., will hold most species of raptor. Precautions are taken to ensure that the line will not break or tear the jesses, consequently setting the bird free. This can be disas-

Figure 10.6 Attaching the creance.

trous for the falconer, rehabilitator, or demonstrator–and fatal to the bird. In addition, the swivel must be removed before attaching the creance. This will ensure that, in the event the creance does break, the bird will at least not have a swivel dangling from the jesses.

Many falconers use the creance only for a short period of time, often just long enough to establish the required pattern of behaviors and responses. The rehabilitator, on the other hand, often needs to use the creance for longer periods. It is therefore imperative that the line be checked frequently for any sign of weakening or fraying. If this is permitted to happen, the

line will eventually snap. Knots in the line will also weaken it, so it is wise to check the line for knots, removing any which are found.

Fishing line can also be used as a creance, but there is always the risk of the line getting tangled in the bird's feet or around its legs, causing serious damage. Over the years I have had many problems with the creance becoming tangled in vegetation. This will happen even after one has inspected the area first and pulled out any obvious clumps of grass or weeds.

Re-winding the creance is another problem. The standard winding stick works, but it is easy to drop the stick. Winding 330 ft. (100 m) of cord is not a simple task, so I prefer to use a large fishing reel, which has an adjustable drag. The reel can be mounted on a portion of fishing rod or aluminum tubing. The drag from the reel and the mount is enough to gently slow a bird down. In the rehabilitation context, it is vital that someone holds the reel or line when the bird is being test flown. The person holding the line must run with the bird and gently slow it down before it takes all of the creance. Gloves are also important for this work; nylon or terylene line will cut the trainer's hands if grabbed barehanded in an effort to stop a eagle or falcon that is out of control and heading rapidly down wind.

Just as leashes are important, so are creances. It is imperative that this equipment is checked every day and every time it is used.

10.7 PERCHES

The question of perches is often a complex issue. Traditionally, falcons have been kept on block perches and hawks on bow perches. In theory, falcons by their nature prefer a flat surface that mimics a rocky outcrop, while hawks prefer a branch-

like perch. It is my experience that this is not always so. I have kept peregrines that preferred a bow perch and goshawks that preferred a block perch. Many African falcons live nowhere near cliffs or rocky gorges, more often than not inhabiting areas where there are trees.

Since more species are now being used for demonstrations and falconry, perch design must vary accordingly. In many respects it is wise to adopt the attitude of "horses for courses" and use the type of perch most suited to the species, or the perch that is preferred by the bird in question. Some modern lathe-turned blocks are incredibly well made, but often they are impractical. The Arab block is not designed to have a bird left on it unattended and, because they are quite tall, the falcon needs to have long jesses and a long leash, which becomes a problem if the bird bates. There is a risk of leg damage if the bird is suddenly drawn to a halt. This can be prevented by using a rubber damper (see Leashes), or by not using the Arab perch.

10.7.1 Block perches

If one wishes to stick to tradition and use blocks for falcons and bow perches for eagles, hawks, and buzzards, then he should follow these basic rules for block perches.

1. Make sure the block perch has a top diameter that is wide enough to prevent the raptor's jesses from straddling it.

2. Make the lower portion of the block slightly narrower than the top diameter. Falcons defecate straight down, and if the block is cylindrical, excrement will collect on the sides.

3. The top should be slightly domed, and covered with astroturf, coco-matting, or something that will not allow the bird to perch flat footed.

4. When using a lathe-turned block, watch for signs of weathering, such as splitting. One does not want a leash getting caught up in a gap on the perch.

5. If using a home welded ring for the leash attachment, check the joint regularly.

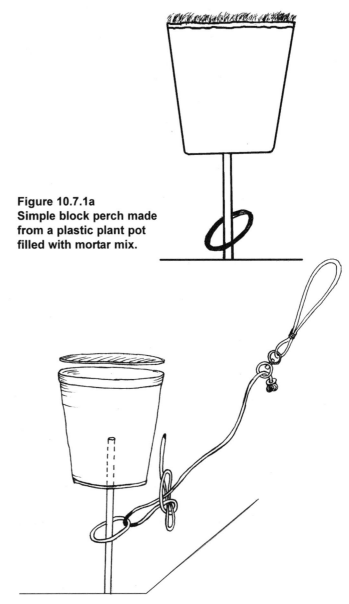

Figure 10.7.1a
Simple block perch made from a plastic plant pot filled with mortar mix.

Figure 10.7.1b
Block perch with an Arab leash attachment.

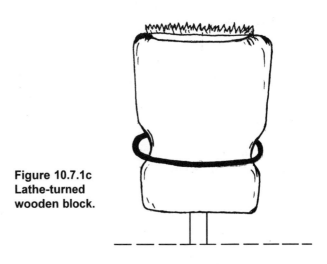

Figure 10.7.1c
Lathe-turned wooden block.

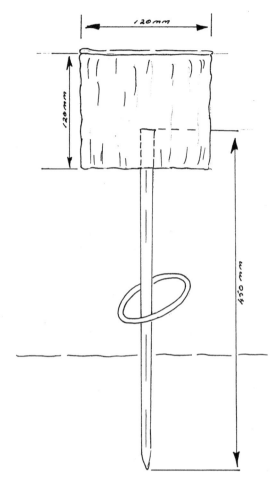

Figure 10.7.1d
Basic block—treated pine with metal stake inserted.

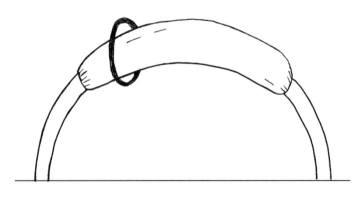

Figure 10.7.2a
Basic steel bow perch.

10.7.2 Bow perches

Bow perches are somewhat different. The ring that holds the leash must be able to slide over the padding at the top of the bow. Padding the top too thickly will only result in the endless problem of having the hawk hanging over the bow with the ring jammed on the padding. I have used a naturally curved branch for a bow perch; this worked fairly well, but the ring would not travel smoothly from one end to the other, and ultimately I had to throw this perch away despite the work that went into it.

All of my current bow perches are made from galvanized piping bent into a bow and then set onto a heavy base plate. These perches can be pegged down if necessary. All of my eagles use enormous blocks, with the option of a large rock nearby. The rock has an irregular shape so the eagles can choose which portion of the rock to use. There are many wonderful variations of bow and block perches, and each has its merits. Regardless of this, almost all falconers and rehabilitators that I know use the standard block and bow perch for most of their birds, including trained owls which should be left loose in a pen.

There are a few more things to remember. The tethered bird is vulnerable. It cannot go anywhere to avoid trouble or to move out of the sun. It cannot untangle itself if it becomes tangled in the leash, or escape its neighbors that may be intent on killing it. In a perfect world, each bird should have a room to itself or be placed on comfortable perches at night, with no risk from its closest neighbor.

If one is experiencing foot problems with his birds, such as bumblefoot (see 8.7, Veterinary aspects), then he is faced with a management problem. Bumblefoot and other associated leg and foot problems invariably have a cause, and it is far easier to prevent rather than treat these problems. Feather damage is another potential threat if the wrong perch is used. The bow perch that ends up with the ring jammed on the padding will cause the leash to run up into the hawk's tail, particularly if the leash is too short. The hawk will be forced to stand on "tiptoes" and the leash will break the deck feathers.

Perches that are placed too close to other obstacles, such as wire mesh, will cause problems. The hawk, falcon, or eagle that is suddenly startled into a bate will hang onto the mesh with its wings and tail outstretched. Bow perches or blocks set on heavy bases and then placed on a concrete or other abrasive surface will destroy a raptor's feet when its bates, even if a mat is laid down. A bow perch placed too close to a wall, so that the hawk's tail comes in constant contact with the wall surface, will inevitably result in a tail covered in excrement.

The use of a block, bow, or ring perch must be accompanied by careful management. Many falconers that fly only a few birds use a free loft system. Their birds are allowed access to water, sun, wind, and shelter, if they want it. They are well manned and can be simply taken up and flown. On the other hand, many zoological institutions that have a flight show or display tether all their birds, largely due to space constraints. It is not conducive to a good show, or to good public relations, to display raptors with damaged or excrement-covered feathers.

As a management tool, in terms of maintaining and retaining a well-behaved and calm-natured trained raptor, tethering is sometimes necessary. The act of picking the bird up and setting it out in the early morning sun so that it has visual access to the trainer's world assists in maintaining the required attitude toward humans. Wild and nervous birds should never be left unattended when tethered in the weathering area, just as they should never be left unattended when hooded. One must be sensitive toward the needs of the bird; properly meeting its perching requirements is vital to it comfort and welfare.

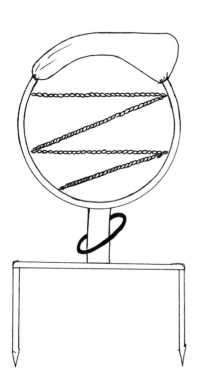

Figure 10.7.2b Ring perch.

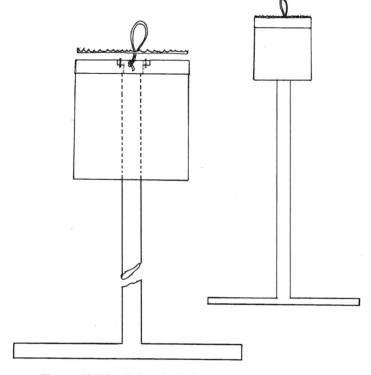

Figure 10.7.2c Pole perch.

10.8 USING BELLS

Bells are wonderful additions for the flying hawk. They allow the trainer to know where the bird is and what it is doing, both in the flying field and weathering area. Bells can either be tail-mounted, leg-mounted, or neck-mounted.

With the advent of the transmitters, bells have become almost superfluous. I say "almost" because I have still located birds by the sound of the bell alone when the transmitter signal was bouncing off electric fences or generally being confusing. One must never be complacent, relying solely upon technology and regarding the transmitter as the be all and end all. Using one bell and one transmitter is ideal, preferably both tail-mounted, as this reduces the amount of gear on the bird's legs. Neck-mounted bells can be used, but only with caution. I used them once many years ago on one of my lanners, but when it caught

a francolin, the latter somehow got its leg underneath the bell attachment, nearly strangling the falcon. Leg bells are subject to similar problems; I have had goshawks caught in dense bush by the bell. Tail bells are unobtrusive and equally effective.

The trainer should not use bells, or hoods, for their aesthetic value alone. If he thinks he needs bells, then he should use them wisely and mount them properly. One can often put the bell on the same mount as the transmitter; it will lie to one side but still have the desired effect. The bells can also be attached directly to the transmitter. The fact that it might touch the transmitter and muffle the sound is of little consequence. Birds undergoing rehabilitation should not wear bells, but the demonstration bird can, and must, wear a bell, particularly in the weathering area.

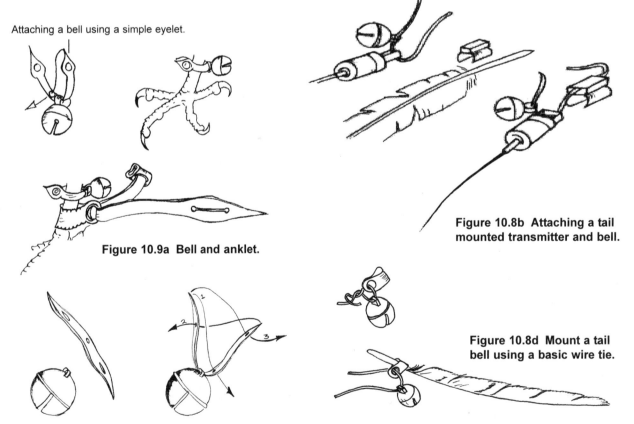

Attaching a bell using a simple eyelet.

Figure 10.9a Bell and anklet.

Figure 10.8b Attaching a tail mounted transmitter and bell.

Figure 10.8d Mount a tail bell using a basic wire tie.

Figure 10.8c Attaching a leg mounted bell.

APPENDIX 1

1.1 Live food production

Breeding rats and mice for use as food is a viable option for those who treat and care for large numbers of injured raptors or other meat-eating birds. Space for breeding cages, the cost of heating a breeding room, and the cost of feeding dozens of rodents all need to be considered. Overall, this will prove cheaper than buying rodents from pet shops, which is not a viable option, as the cost will add up very quickly if you are feeding growing raptors. One should calculate the amounts being used and then weigh up the costs.

We maintain 50 rodent boxes and produce about 300 mice per week. Even that is not enough to feed our existing number of raptors. We also breed pigeons and purchase day-old chickens, freshly killed and then frozen.

1.2 Breeding rats and mice and other food animals

Stocking rates: 1 male/2–6 females
Housing Temperature: 18–27C (64.4–80.6F)
Box size: 7 x 14 x 18 in. (18 x 35 x 45 cm)

Each adult rat should have at least 240 cm2 of floor space, and females should be removed from the communal breeding boxes before they give birth, and then returned after the young have been weaned. Each female should be allowed to produce eight litters before being "retired." The average number of young born normally declines after about eight litters. This general rule applies to mice as well as to rats.

General Biology
Mating age: 8–12 weeks
Breeding season: continuous
Weaning age: 21 days
Litter size: 6–12

It is not worthwhile breeding quail, as the maintenance of breeding units is invariably quite high. If quail are raised locally on a commercial basis, arrangements might be made to obtain a steady supply at a reasonable cost. Otherwise, day-old chickens can be purchased and grown out for a few weeks; these are just as good as quail in some cases.

Pigeons, either trapped as feral or purchased from markets, can be deadly. Many feral pigeons carry trichomoniasis, a protozoan disease that kills raptors in a very short time. If pigeons are being bred, then they should be treated for any transmittable disease on a regular basis. Freshly killed pigeons should be frozen for six weeks before use, and then it is advisable to remove the head and crop. For use as a feeder bird, it is probably not economically viable to breed pigeons. However, there is no harm in having a loft where one can produce ten or twenty pigeons every six weeks.

1.3 Freezing food before use and using road kills

Some animals carry parasites. It is always advisable to check all animals that have been picked up, shot, or bred before using them. Road kills are a good source of food, but using freshly killed birds picked up off the road is not a good idea; always freeze them before use. Most countries have enacted laws that prevent anyone from legally picking up dead native animals, let alone using them for food, and even though one may have a permit to care for sick or injured native wildlife, he is often not permitted to recover wildlife that is dead.

If road kills are available, remember to freeze any carcass first. It is not fully understood just what portion of any wild raptor population succumbs to parasites or what percentage of prey items caught and killed carry potentially harmful parasites.

Feather mites are one thing, but infestations of worms and other nasty "insurgents" are a different matter altogether. Feeding pigeons and starlings to captive raptors is a serious threat if they are not treated correctly. In some areas starlings and feral pigeons can be trapped in large numbers and killed, but it is imperative that the bodies are frozen before being used for food. In the case of pigeons, they should be kept alive and treated for any parasite before being culled and frozen prior to use. In a recent sample of 100 pigeons that were trapped and removed from three different buildings, 45 of the birds were carrying Trichomoniasis. From this example, it is possible to extrapolate the overall carrying rate among the entire feral pigeon population and hazard a guess as to the number of raptors that must die each year from eating infected pigeons.

There is no substitute for good food preparation. If one is going to use road kills, then he must check them first, prior to freezing. Again, pigeons should be treated for a few weeks before being culling and frozen. Just as good food is important for humans, so it is for the meat-eating raptor.

Appendix 2

2.1 Putting rehabilitation and foraging in context

I have always been intrigued by the success of the hunt when carried out by either predatory birds or predatory mammals. At one stage, while flying a lanner falcon I watched a pride of lions kill a buffalo not more than one kilometer from where I sat with my falcon feeding off her own kill. It was the mechanics of these hunts that made them interesting, not the kill.

In the rehabilitation context, it is the combination of these two components that is important, the search strategy and the final attack that ends in a kill. For the rehabilitator, the failure to kill is a cause for concern, especially after an apparently easy opportunity. The researcher must also have an insight into the dynamics of a hunt, particularly when trying to assess foraging efficiency in terms of a hunt/kill ratio. The perspective of the falconer, who has spent years flying various species of raptors, differs; to him, it is the style of the attack that is important, and the kill is a mere by-product of the flight (thus, if a peregrine kills a duck from a low pitch after a pathetic stoop, the value of the flight is reduced considerably). Regardless of this, there is much to be learned from the trained raptor pertaining to the manner in which it selects, pursues, and finally kills its prey.

Prey selection is obviously important. Becoming "wedded" to certain prey types is a by-product of success and/or prey abundance. I have kept records of success rates, prey species selected, and the number of flights observed for many of the birds I have flown over the years. Some of these statistics date back to 1979. I have put them into tables for interest. These tables include observations made in both Zimbabwe and Australia.

It is interesting to note that the first goshawk, in Table A.1, showed no hesitation in pursuing large birds, even up to his own weight, whereas the male in the Table A.2 was reluctant to pursue anything heavier than 70 grams.

As a further comparison, I have added a list of observations made in the vicinity of a Gabar goshawk nest (Table A.3). The breeding male was monitored for 3 hours and the number of attacks at prey and the prey species were recorded. At the time of observation, the female was brooding three chicks, so the hunting attempts and success of the male was influenced by the hungry brood. The male brought prey to the nest every 20 minutes, on average.

Table A.1 Hunt success rates over 15 days for a hand-raised male Gabar goshawk, Zimbabwe (Richard Naisbitt). This bird was given maintenance feed when unsuccessful during a hunt.

Prey species	Number of chases	Number of kills	Success	Prey weight (g)
Fiscal shrike	7	1	14%	60
Harlequin quail	16	31	8%	65
Coucal	2	1	50%	180
Turtle doves	9	0	0	180
Firefinches	18	6	33%	10
Mousebird	5	1	20%	55
Wattled starling	11	1	9%	80
Glossy starling	2	0	0	
Tawny-flanked prinia	10	2	20%	7
Fiery-necked nightjar	1	1	100%	48
Bronze-winged courser	3	1	33%	98
Red-billed quelea	6	2	33%	28
Red bishop	2	1	50%	35
Pintailed whydah	5	1	20%	16
House sparrow	13	5	38%	33
Total chases	**110**			
Total kills		**26**		
Total prey weight				**895**
Total success %			**23%**	

Table A.2 Hunt success rates over 10 days for a parent-raised Gabar goshawk, Zimbabwe. (Richard Naisbitt)

Prey species	Number of chases	Number of kills	Success %	Prey weight
Harlequin quail	3	1	33	65
Firefinch	7	4	57	10
Fiscal shrike	2	0	0	
Red bishop	12	5	41	35
House sparrow	14	9	64	22
Mousebird	3	1	33	48
Tawny-flanked prinia1	1	100	8	
Pintailed whydah	6	2	33	17
Scaly-feathered finch	11	7	63	12
Rattling cisticola	3	1	33	8
Total chases	**62**			
Total Kills		**31**		
Total prey weight				**225**
Total success			**50%**	

The Gabar goshawk in the above table was hand raised and flown for one season before he was killed. I have flown a number of these birds in the falconry context, and the next table highlights the differences between the success rates of a hand-raised male and a trapped, parent-raised male.

Table A.3 Hunt success of a breeding male Gabar goshawk, Zimbabwe (Richard Naisbitt).

Prey species visible	Attacks	Number of attacks	Number captured	Success %	Prey weight
Tawny-flanked prinia	yes	6	3	50	8
Firefinch					
House sparrow	yes	10	1	10	22
Mousebird	yes	4	1	25	48
Scaly-feathered finch					
Hump-tailed whydah					
Cape white-eye					
Three-streaked tchagra	yes	12	1	8	33
Fiscal shrike					
Red-backed shrike					
Kirk's agama*	yes	2	2	100	30
Wahlberg's skink					
Single-striped mouse	yes	3	1	33	60
Total hunts	**37**				
Total kills			**9**		
Total prey weight					**247 g**
Total success				**24%**	

This wild male had no human assistance in his hunts, as would a trained bird, but even then he did amazingly well, which is the hallmark of the adult. All three chicks fledged, a further sign of foraging proficiency.

Table A.4 refers to a pair of brown goshawks in southeastern Australia. They were observed foraging over a period of 15 hours. Both birds were feeding two nearly fledged young. This area has a different environment, both in terms of climate and habitat, to that of the gabar goshawks referred to above.

Table A.4   Foraging success of a pair of Australian brown goshawks, southeastern Australia (Richard Naisbitt 1997).

Prey available	Male goshawk	Female goshawk	Number of attacks	Success	Prey weight (g)
Rabbit*		Yes	0/3	0/1	0/400
Noisy miner	Yes		1/0	1/0	60/0
Indian mynah*	Yes	Yes	0/1	0/1	0/75
Moorhen		Yes	0/1	0/1	0/400
Turtle dove*		Yes	0/4	0/0	
Wattle bird		Yes	0/3	0/1	0/75
Eastern rosella	Yes		4/0	1/0	75/0
Rail	Yes		9/0	1/0	125/0
King parrot	Yes	Yes	2/6	0/0	
Blackbird*	Yes	Yes	3/1	1/0	60/0
Feral pigeon*		Yes	0/1	0/1	0/350

* Introduced species.

Female's Total attacks / total kills	**20/5**
Male's Total attacks/ total kills	**20/4**
Total female prey weights	**1300 grams**
Total male prey weights	**320 grams**

Female's average prey mass/ hunt	**65 grams**
Male's average prey mass/ hunt	**16 grams**

Female's average body weight	**600 grams**
Male's average body weight	**320 grams**

Hunting statistics are informative and thought provoking when compiled for comparative purposes, particularly when those relating to trained raptors are compared with those relating to wild birds.

In 1986 I released a female lanner into an area which supported 110 species of birds, 68 of which were accessible to the falcon as potential prey. This falcon stayed within the release area for 9 weeks (63 days). The following tables, A.5, A.6, and A.7, give some indication of this particular bird's hunting success over a 30 day period, during which the falcon was observed for two 90 minute periods each day, the first at 6:00 am and the last at 17:00 pm. The first period coincided with first true light, when many species of bird were either leaving roosting areas or were displaying in exposed areas. The last period of the day coincided with a return to roosting areas or an influx of birds to watering points.

Table A.5 Lanner falcon's hunt success, 6:00 AM–7:30 AM, 17 September, Zimbabwe (Richard Naisbitt).

Species	Search strategy	Attack Strategy	Attempts	Success	Success %
Capped wheatear	Still-hunt	Direct attack	3	0	0
Grey hornbill	Still-hunt	Direct attack	11	1	9%

Weight of prey killed	**230 grams**
Percentage of falcon's body weight	**45 %**

Table A.6 Lanner falcon's hunt success, 17:00 PM - 18:30 PM, 18 September, Zimbabwe (Richard Naisbitt).

Species	Search strategy	Attack Strategy	Attempts	Success	Success %
Bronze-winged courser	Prospecting	Tail-chase	1	0	
Cape turtle dove	Still-hunt	Direct attack	11	0	
Red-billed quelea	Still-hunt	Direct attack/tail-chase	16	16%	
Wattled plover	Still-hunt	Direct hunt/tail-chase	1	0	

Weight of prey killed	**28 grams**
Percentage of falcon's body weight	**5%**

Table A.7 Lanner falcon's hunt success, 17:00 PM–18:30 PM, 23 September, Zimbabwe (Richard Naisbitt).

Species	Search Strategy	Attack Strategy	Attempts	Success	Success %
Grey hornbill	Soaring	Stoop/tail-chase	2	0	
Sandgrouse	Still-hunt	Direct attack	1	0	
Red-billed quelea	Still-hunt	Direct attack/tail-chase	9	2	22%
Cape turtle dove	Still-hunt	Direct attack	5	1	20%
Weight of prey killed	**206 grams**				
Percentage of body weight	**41%**				

This particular lanner improved in efficiency in terms of kills/hunt as she gained more experience. Prey selection became more specific; near the end of the 9 week period, 88% of all attacks were made on cape turtle doves. Attack strategies also changed. The direct attack became less frequent in the afternoons, to be replaced by stooping from a low soaring position or a direct attack from a soaring position. This is in contrast to her kill/hunt rate while being flown; Table A.8 gives some indication of her proficiency in the falconry field.

Table A.8   Hunt success rate of a Lanner falcon under controlled conditions over 4 days. June 1986, Zimbabwe (Richard Naisbitt).

Species	Search strategy	Attack strategy	Attempts	Success	Success%
Crested francolin	Soaring	Stoop/tail-chase	3	1	33%
Lilac-breasted roller	Soaring	Stoop	4	2	50%
Arrow-marked babbler	Still-hunt	Tail-chase	1	1	100%
Sandgrouse	Soaring	Stoop	9	0	0
Total weight of prey		**625 grams**			
Percentage of body weight		**122%**			

Comparing foraging strategies between trained birds of various age groups helps in formulating methods suitable for the reintroduction of raptors that have been orphaned, injured, or found in low body condition. It is important to stress the necessity of correctly identifying the species one is dealing with, and ascertaining its foraging methods. Without this knowledge, little can be achieved, or at best, only marginal success can be attained.

This attempt to achieve success in rehabilitation leads to a whole series of new questions, such as the relative value of rehabilitation in terms of its relationship with conservation. The link between conservation and rehabilitation, particularly when one deals with common species, is rather hazy. The amount of money that is spent on the care and treatment of common raptorial birds is astounding, and there is often very little tangible evidence of true success. Common raptorial birds invariably make up the bulk of raptors treated by rehabilitation centers throughout the world. Kestrels are common patients in Europe, Australia, and North America. This is further complicated by the number of birds lost from aviaries, or by falconers or demonstrators.

The Independent Bird Register in the United Kingdom maintains a list of lost and found birds. At the time of writing, there were 350 birds listed on their website, of which none had been claimed. This number was comprised of 28 species, of which only 8 were indigenous to the United Kingdom. It should be mentioned that the Independent Bird Register reunites about 20 birds with their owners per month, but only those people who are registered list their losses. The following table (Table A.9) highlights the species of raptor lost in the United Kingdom. The word lost is used in a general sense, as some of the birds were lost from aviaries and not during free flight displays or in the hunting field.

Table A.9 Birds listed as found on the Independent Bird Register, June 1999.

Owls/eagle owls	Eagles	Falcons	Hawks/buzzards	Sea eagles
Barn 56	Tawny 2	Gyr 14	Harris 99	European 1
Boobook 1	Lanner 115	Red-tailed 45	Bald 1	
European eagle 7	Saker 81	Ferruginous 6		
Snowy 1	Peregrine 85	Cooper's 3		
Tawny 2	Merlin 3	Goshawk 28		
Turkmanian 1	Barbary 3	Sparrowhawk 21		
Bengal 3	Lagger 9	Common 23		
	Kestrel 54			
	Prairie 4			
	Hobby 1			

The number of birds lost and the number of birds bred in captivity, compared to the number of birds rehabilitated, should be examined. The Bird of Prey Trust in the United Kingdom is a private organization that does some excellent work in the rehabilitation and education field. Their rehabilitation statistics for the years 1997 and 1998 are shown in Tables A.10 and A.11.

Statistics compiled by Raptor Rescue, United Kingdom, are shown in Table A.12.

Table A.10 Raptors rehabilitated 1997. Bird of Prey Trust.

Species	Number	Died	Released	Returned to owner
Little owl	19	109		
Tawny owl	24	13	11	
Barn owl	7	6	1	
Kestrel	18	7	11	
Hobby	1	1		
Saker	1			1

Table A.11 Raptors rehabilitated 1998. Bird of Prey Trust.

Species	Number	Died	Released	Returned to owner	Retained
Tawny owl	2714	13			
Little owl	22	14	8		
Barn owl	9	8	1		
Sparrowhawk	8	3	5		
Kestrel	29	9	20		
Hobby	2	1			1
Harrier	1	1			
Buzzard	1			1	

Table A.12 Raptors treated by Raptor Rescue (United Kingdom) 1993–1996 annual surveys.

Species	1993-1994	1994-1995	1995-1996	Total	Total domestic bred raptors
Tawny owl	61	90	108	259	103
Long-eared owl	2	3		5	
Little owl	38	30	30	98	
Barn owl	19	20	12	51	
Short-eared owl	1	2		3	
Peregrine	7	2	3	12	
Merlin	1	2	2	5	
Kestrel	86	54	39	179	
Hobby	3	3	1	7	
Goshawk		1	2	3	
Common buzzard	18	15	2	35	
Rough-legged buzzard		2		2	
Red kite		1		1	
Sparrowhawk	54	54	45	153	
Total birds treated	**290**	**279**	**244**	**813**	

The Bird of Prey Trust and Raptor Rescue are not the only two organizations in the United Kingdom. There are many smaller centers that rehabilitate raptors, and in 1990 there were 230 licensed rehabilitators (Fox 1995). The number of falcons bred in the United Kingdom are highlighted in the next table.

Table A.13 Number and species of falcons bred in captivity over 5 years (Fox 1995).

Species	1988	1989	1990	1991	1992
Lanner falcon	100	75	80	100	125
Lugger falcon	15	25	15	25	25
Prairie falcon	15	20	15	20	20
Saker falcon	30	50	75	90	115
Kestrel	1000	950	775	675	650
Peregrine	175	250	290	315	300

An estimated 1230 individual raptors were treated in 1990, of which 580 were subsequently released. From 1980–1991, a total of 23,804 diurnal raptors were bred in the United Kingdom alone. Many of these species were common indigenous species or common in their native habitats. The situation is different in Australia, where few species are regularly bred in captivity but the trend of rehabilitating all species remains the same. Of Australia's 24 diurnal species of raptor, only 5 species are being bred on a regular basis, and only by two institutions. The situation regarding owls differs, with 5 out of 8 species being bred on a regular basis. It is ironic that the 5 species to which I refer are common, and frequently seen in rehabilitation statistics, whereas the other 3 are relatively scarce, or limited in their natural range.

In the state of Victoria, Australia, there are an estimated 300 wildlife care operators, some of whom receive and care for raptors. One of the major problems with compiling statistics in Australia is poor or inaccurate identification of the birds that are treated, and this in turn leads to incorrect or poorly implemented release strategies. Training of wildlife care operators is imperative. This applies to many other countries and their wildlife care groups as well.

The following table indicates the number of raptors treated by one wildlife rehabilitator, Michelle Manhal, who specializes in raptors, for which she has excellent facilities.

Table A.14 Raptors rehabilitated in Victoria, May 1996–May 1999 (Michelle Manhal, pers. comm).

Species	Juvenile	Adult	Retained	Died	Euthanased	Released
Peregrine	7	14	8	2	7	4
Hobby	9	4	1	1	5	6
Kestrel	21	10		3	11	17
Brown falcon	10	9	3	1	5	10
Brown goshawk	13	4		3	9	5
Wedge-tailed eagle	22	9	6	1	17	7
Total	**82**	**50**	**18**	**11**	**54**	**49**
% released:	**37%**					

Of these raptors, 37% were presented for treatment after having been injured by colliding with vehicles. Wedge-tailed eagles are particularly vulnerable to such collisions. A large number of raptors is treated in the state of Victoria, Australia, by a state government organization. Table A.15 gives an indication of the admission and subsequent release rates of birds cared for by this institution.

Table A.15　Raptors rehabilitated by Healesville Sanctuary, Victoria, Australia, Jan. 1994–May 1995.

Species	Number	Released	Died	Euthanized	Retained
Boobook owl	14	2	2	10	
Barn owl	6	4	1		1
Peregrine falcon	12	3		6	3
Hobby	14	7		6	1
Black falcon	4	3			1
Brown falcon	6	2	1	2	1
Kestrel	6	4	2		
Black-shouldered kite	11	3	1	7	
Collared sparrowhawk	4	4			
Brown goshawk	15	2		8	5
Little eagle	2	1			1
Sea eagle	1				1
Wedge-tailed eagle	10	3	2		5
Marsh harrier	5	4		1	

Total: 110

% released: 26%

For comparison, the next tables give an indication of the numbers of raptors rehabilitated in the United States of America by the Minnesota Raptor Center.

Table A.16　Raptors in care at the Minnesota Raptor Center. Jan. 1995.

Owls	Eagles	Hawks	Falcons	Buzzards
Great horned 11	Bald 16	Sharp-shinned 1	Peregrine 9	Red-tailed 27
Barred owl 5	Golden 2	Cooper's 3	Kestrel 5	Broad-winged 4
Saw-whet owl 4			Merlin 1	Rough-legged 2
Snowy owl 1				Swainson's 1
Short-eared owl 1				
Long-eared owl 1				

As mentioned earlier, there are certain species that frequently appear in statistics, either because of their common population status, their foraging strategies, or a combination of the two.

Table A.17   Raptors in care at the Minnesota Raptor Center, Jan. 1996.

Owls	Eagles	Hawks	Falcons	Buzzards	Other
Great horned 11	Golden 2	Sharp-shinned 1	Peregrine 9	Red-tailed 20	Osprey 2
Screech 1	Bald 13		Kestrel 8	Rough-legged 1	
Barred 9			Merlin 1		
Saw-whet 2					
Short-eared 1					
Snowy 1					

Many centers experience an increase in the number of patients during winter or late spring, reflecting the times when juveniles are finding it difficult to make it through the winter or are just fledging. These trends appear worldwide.

The Bird of Prey Foundation is another comparatively large raptor center which deals with and rehabilitates large numbers of raptors every year. In 1999, they admitted their 6000 th patient, a considerable feat. The 1997 rehabilitation statistics for the Bird of Prey Foundation appear below.

Table A.18   Raptors rehabilitated in 1997 by the Bird of Prey Foundation. Sigrid Uelblacker (pers. comm).

Falcons	Hawks	Buzzards	Eagles	Owls	Other
American kestrels 112	Cooper's 13	Swainson's 35	Golden 7	Barn 6	Turkey vulture 3
Crested caracara 1	Sharp-shinned 14	Rough-legged 3	Bald 3	Boreal 1	Hybrid falcon 1
Merlin 4		Red-tailed 27		Burrowing 9	Harrier 1*
Peregrine 4		Ferruginous 13		Great-horned 52	
Prairie 11				Long-eared 9	
				Screech 12	
				Saw-whet 8	
				Pygmy 1	
				Flammulated 1	

The task of raptor rehabilitation is often seen as the process of treatment, but in reality one cannot avoid the repercussions of releasing a raptor into a potentially hostile environment. Very few centers have the financial resources to actively monitor all of the raptors they release. Recovery from banding is an unreliable means of confirming survival, as it relies upon the bird being picked up, checked, and then reported. The true sign of success is the integration of a rehabilitated bird back into the breeding population, either that from which it originally came or one which it joined after release. There are, of course, other variables. For example, it is difficult to judge when a bird is suffering from old age. When dealing with a migratory species, the ramifications for an individual bird are great; will it migrate, and if it does, will it survive? Will it attempt to breed, and if so, will it successfully rear young?

The only eagle that was monitored via satellite (PTT) in Australia died after six weeks. Its death was due to starvation or aggressive interaction with wild eagles. A total of $A10,000 dollars was spent on the eagle, excluding veterinary costs. In the end, we learned very little other than the difficulties faced by rehabilitated eagles.

As mentioned earlier, banding recovery is unreliable in assessing long term survivability. The Liberty Wildlife Rehabilitation Foundation in Central Arizona received 1,289 raptors for care over an eight year period. Kathy Ingram, in her paper "Survival and Movement of Rehabilitated Raptors" (South West Raptor Management Symposium and Workshop. 1985) gives a breakdown of the banding recoveries from a total of 434 individual raptors which were banded, comprising 10 species. Barn owls made up the bulk of the birds banded. From this group, 41 banded birds were recovered, a recovery rate of 9.4%, representing 8 species. Red-tailed hawks, barn owls, and great-horned owls were recovered most frequently.

Two basic handicaps predisposed many the raptors released to being recovered: "Tameness" proved to be a disability or handicap, as did neurological damage. These two factors are serious, and no bird should be released if it has one or both of these handicaps. On the other hand, some of the birds that were banded and released had other significant disabilities. A red-tailed hawk was released with one leg, and subsequently survived for six months before being recovered dead after moving only six kilometers. A prairie falcon that had suffered a fractured coracoid survived only three weeks following release. The study highlighted, perhaps inadvertently, the difficulties experienced by the more dynamic raptors, or raptors that use a complex and strenuous attack strategy, especially when one considers that the study itself included a relatively small representation of typical attacking raptors.

The arguments will continue regarding the objectives of rehabilitation. Survival is one goal of the rehabilitator, but ultimately, the need to return a viable survivor and potential breeding bird should be the primary objective. To achieve this, it is imperative that good release preparation is carried out, accompanied by good veterinary care. Large rehabilitation centers, which have access to all the resources necessary for proper rehabilitation, invariably offer a better chance of releasing viable survivors. The small backyard rehabilitators are often toiling at a disadvantage, either through a lack of resources or through inexperience in dealing with complicated cases. We cannot avoid the fact that many of the raptors treated are common species, with a wide distribution, and are therefore often encountered. Good raptor management is not confined to the rehabilitator, but also extends to the falconer and zookeeper who hopes or strives to achieve and maintain a healthy captive raptor.

Table A.19   Foraging strategies of mixed raptor genera.

Scientific name	Common name	Searcher	Attacker	Diet
Aviceda cuculoides	African baza or Cuckoo falcon	Yes	No	Frogs/insects
Circus ranivoris	African marsh-harrier	Yes	No	Mammals/Birds/ amphibians
Melierax metabates	Dark chanting-goshawk	Yes	Yes*	Mammals/birds/ reptiles
Kaupifalco monogrammicus	Lizard buzzard	Yes	No	Rodents/birds/reptiles
Falco biarmicus	Lanner falcon	Yes*	Yes	Birds/mammals/insects
F. peregrinus minor	African peregrine	No	Yes	Birds/insects
F. mexicanus	Prairie falcon	Yes*	Yes	Birds/mammals/ reptiles
F. rusticolis	Gyr falcon	No	Yes	Birds/mammals
F. cherrug	Saker falcon	Yes	Yes	Birds/mammals/ insects
Micrastur ruficollis	Barred forest-falcon	Yes	No	Reptiles/mammals
F. rufigularis	Bat falcon	No	Yes	Bats/birds
Accipiter superciliosus	Tiny hawk	Yes	Yes	Birds/insects
Parabuteo unicinctus	Harris hawk	Yes*	Yes	Birds/reptiles/ mammals
Sagittarius serpentarius	Secretary bird	Yes	No	Mammals/reptiles/ insects

REFERENCES

Aguilar, R.F., V.E. Smith, P. Ogburn and P.T. Redig. 1995. Arrhythmias associated with isoflurane anesthesia in bald eagles (Haliaeetus leucocephalus). J. Zoo Wildl. Med. 26: 508–516.

Anderson, R.C. 1992. The superfamily Diplotriaenoidea. Pp. 523–527 in Nematode Parasites of Vertebrates, Their Development and Transmission. CAB International, Wallingford, Oxon, UK.

Barton, N.W. and D.C. Houston. 1996. Factors influencing the size of some internal organs in raptors. J. Raptor Res. 30: 219–223.

Bennett, R.A., M.J. Yaeger, A. Trapp and R.C. Cambre. 1997. Histologic evaluation of the tissue reaction to five suture materials in the body wall of rock doves (Columbia livia). J. Avian Med. Surg. 11: 175–182.

Beyer, W.N., G.H. Heinz and A.W. Redmon-Norwood (eds.) 1996. Environmental Contaminants in Wildlife: Interpreting Tissue Concentrations. CRC Press Inc., Boca Raton, Florida.

Brown, R.E. and R.D. Klemm. 1990. Surgical anatomy of the propatagium. Proc. Assoc. Avian Vet. Pp. 176–181.

Burn, J.D. and F.A. Leighton. 1996. Further studies of brain cholinesterase : cholinergic receptor ratios in the diagnosis of acute lethal poisoning of birds by anticholinesterase pesticides. J. Wildl. Dis. 32: 216–224.

Cade,T.J. 1982. Falcons of the World. William Collins Sons and Co. Limited, London.

Chaplin, S.B. 1990. Guidelines for exercise in rehabilitated raptors. Wildl. J. 12: 17–20.

Chaplin, S.B., L.R. Mueller and L.A. Degernes. 1993. Physiological assessment of rehabilitated raptors prior to release. Pp. 167–173 in Redig et al. (eds.), Raptor Biomedicine.

Clum, N.J., M.P. Fitzpatrick and E.S. Dierenfeld. 1996. Effects of diet on nutritional content of whole vertebrate prey. Zoo Biol. 15: 525–537.

Cooper, J.E. and L. Gibson. 1980. The assessment of health in casualty birds of prey intended for release. Vet. Rec. 106: 340–341.

Cooper, J.E., and A.G. Greenwood (eds.).1981 Recent Advances in the Study of Raptor Diseases. Chiron Publications Ltd., Keighley, West Yorkshire, England.

Davidson, M. 1997. Ocular consequences of trauma in raptors. Seminars in Avian and Exotic Pet Medicine 6: 121–130.

Degernes, L.A. 1994. Trauma medicine. Pp. 417–433 in B.W. Ritchie et al. (eds.), Avian Medicine: Principles and Application.

Dierenfeld, E.S., M.P. Fitzpatrick, T.C. Douglas and S.A. Dennison. 1996. Mineral concentrations in whole mice and rats used as food. Zoo Biol. 15: 83–88.

Dierenfeld, E.S., C.E. Sandfort and W.C. Satterfield. 1989. Influence of diet on plasma Vitamin E in captive peregrine falcons. J. Wildl. Manage. 53: 160–164.

Dierenfeld, E.S. and M.G. Traber. 1992. Vitamin E status of exotic animals compared with livestock and domestics. Pp. 345–370 in L. Packer and J. Fuchs (eds.), Vitamin E in Health and Disease.

Duke, G.E., P.T. Redig and W. Jones. 1981. Recoveries and resightings of released rehabilitated raptors. Raptor Res. 15: 97–107.

Dumonceaux, G. and G.J. Harrison. 1994. Toxins. Pp. 1030–1052 in B.W. Ritchie et al. (eds.), Avian Medicine: Principles and Application.

Ephrati, C. and J.T. Lumeij. 1997. Rectal fluid therapy in birds – an experimental study. J. Avian Med. Surg. 11: 4–6.

Erickson, H.H., C.S. Lundin, B.K. Erickson and J.R. Coffman. 1991. Indices of performance in the racing quarter horse. Eq. Exercise Physiol. 3: 41–46.

Ferrer, M. and F. Hiraldo. 1995. Human-associated Staphylococcal infection in Spanish Imperial Eagles. J. Wildl. Dis. 31: 534–536.

Fix, A.S. and S.Z. Barrows. 1990. Raptors rehabilitated in Iowa during 1986 and 1987: a retrospective study. J. Wildl. Dis. 26: 18–21.

Fowler, M.E. (ed.). 1993. Zoo and Wild Animal Medicine, Current Therapy 3. W.B. Saunders Company, Philadelphia, Pennsylvania.

Fox, N. 1995. Understanding the Bird of Prey. Hancock House Publishers Ltd., Surrey, BC, and Blaine, Washington.

Gerlach, H. 1994. Viruses. Pp. 862–948 in B.W. Ritchie et al. (eds.), Avian Medicine: Principles and Application.

Glinski, R.L., B.G. Pendleton, M.B. Moss, M.N. LeFranc, Jr., B.A. Millsap and S.W. Hoffmann (eds.) 1988. Rehabilitated Raptors. Scientific Technical Series no. 11. National Wildlife Federation, Washington, D.C.

Hamilton, L.L., P.J. Zwank and G.H. Olsen. 1988. Movements and survival of released rehabilitated hawks. J. Raptor Res. 22: 22–26.

Hill, E.F. 1988. Brain cholinesterase activity of apparently normal wild birds. J. Wildl. Dis. 24: 51–61.

Holz, P.H. and R. Naisbitt. 1999. Fitness level as a determining factor in the survival of rehabilitated raptors released back into the wild – preliminary results. In J.T. Lumeij et al. (eds.) Raptor Biomedicine II. In press.

Ingram, K. 1988. Survival and movements of rehabilitated raptors. Pp. 277–281 in R.L. Glinski et al. (eds.), Rehabilitated Raptors.

Jones, W.E. 1989. Selecting and conditioning the equine athlete. Pp. 281–317 in   Equine Sports Medicine. Lea and Febiger, Philadelphia, Pennsylvania.

Kanowski, J. 1998. The abundance of Rufous owls in upland and highland rainforest of North- east Queensland. Emu 98 (1): 58–61.

Kaufman, G.E., J.R. Paul-Murphy and M. Finnegan. 1993. Preliminary evaluation of the effects of dexamethasone on serum hepatic enzymes, glucose, and total protein in red-tailed hawks. Pp. 184–187 in P.T. Redig et al. (eds.), Raptor Biomedicine.

Knuth, S.T. and S.B. Chaplin. 1994. The effect of exercise on plasma activities of lactate dehydrogenase and creatine kinase in red-tailed hawks (Buteo jamaicensis). J. Raptor Res. 28: 27–33.

LaBonde, J. 1991. Avian toxicology. Veterinary Clinics of North America Small Animal Practice 21: 1329–1341.

Liptak, J.M. 1997. An overview of the topical management of wounds. Aust. Vet. J. 75: 408–413.

Lumeij, J.T., P.T. Redig, J.D. Remple, J.E. Cooper and M. Lierz (eds.) 1999. Raptor Biomedicine II. Abu Dhabi Printing and Publishing Company, Mina, Abu Dhabi, UAE. In press.

Maclean, G.L. 1984. Robert's Birds of Southern Africa. The John Voelcker Bird Book Fund, Cape Town, South Africa.

Marchant, S. and P.J. Higgins. 1993. Handbook of Australian, New Zealand & Antarctic Birds, Volume 2. Oxford University Press, Melbourne, Australia.

Martell, M., P. Redig, J. Nibe and G. Buhl. 1991. Survival and movements of released rehabilitated bald eagles. J. Raptor Res. 25: 72–76.

Martin, H.D., K.A. Bruecker, D.D. Herrick and J. Scherpelz. 1993. Elbow luxations in raptors: a review of eight cases. Pp. 199–206 in P.T. Redig et al. (eds.), Raptor Biomedicine.

Martin, H. and B.W. Ritchie. 1994. Orthopedic surgical techniques. Pp. 1137–1169 in B.W. Ritchie et al. (eds), Avian Medicine: Principles and Application.

Mikaelian, I., I. Paillet and D. Williams. 1994. Comparative use of various mydriatic drugs in kestrels (Falco tinnunculus). Am. J. Vet. Res. 55: 270–272.

Mooney, N. 1994. Proposed ARA guidelines for the rehabilitation of raptors. Aust. Raptor Assoc. News. 15: 57–67.

Morishita, T.Y., A.T. Fullerton, L.J. Lowenstine, I.A. Gardner and D.L. Brooks. 1998. Morbidity and mortality in free-living raptorial birds of Northern California: a retrospective study, 1983–1994. J. Avian Med. Surg. 12: 78–81.

Murphy, C.J. 1987. Raptor ophthalmology. Compendium on Continuing Education 9: 241–260.

Naisbitt, R. 1998. Rehabilitating raptors – surviving after release. Thylacinus 22: 7–16.

Needham, J.R. 1981. Bacterial flora of birds of prey. Pp. 3–9 in J.E. Cooper and A.G. Greenwood (eds.), Recent Advances in the Study of Raptor Diseases.

Olsen, P. 1995. Australian Birds of Prey, The Biology and Ecology of Raptors. University of New South Wales Press, Sydney, Australia

Orosz, S.E., P.K. Ensley and C.J. Haynes. 1992. Avian Surgical Anatomy, Thoracic and Pelvic Limbs. W.B. Saunders Company, Philadelphia, Pennsylvania.

Packer, L. and J. Fuchs (eds.) 1992. Vitamin E in Health and Disease. Marcel Dekker Inc., New York, New York.

Parry-Jones,J. 1991. Falconry: Care, Captive Breeding and Conservation. David and Charles, Devon, England.

Peirce, M.A. 1981. Current knowledge of the haematozoa of raptors. Pp. 15–19 in J.E. Cooper and A.G. Greenwood (eds.), Recent Advances in the Study of Raptor Diseases.

Phalen, D.N., M.E. Mitchell and M.L. Cavazos-Martinez. 1996. Evaluation of three heat sources for their ability to maintain core body temperature in the anesthetized avian patient. J. Avian Med. Surg. 10: 174–178.

Porter, S.L. 1993. Pesticide poisoning in birds of prey. Pp. 239–245 in P.T. Redig et al. (eds.), Raptor Biomedicine.

Prijono, W.B. and F.A. Leighton. 1991. Parallel measurement of brain acetylcholinesterase and the muscarinic cholinergic receptor in the diagnosis of acute, lethal poisoning by anti- cholinesterase pesticides. J. Wildl. Dis. 27: 110–115.

Redig, P.T. 1993a. Medical Management of Birds of Prey. 3rd ed. The Raptor Center, University of Minnesota, St. Paul.

Redig, P.T. 1993b. Bumblefoot treatment in raptors. Pp. 181–188 in M.E. Fowler (ed.), Zoo and Wild Animal Medicine, Current Therapy 3.

Redig, P.T. 1993c. Avian aspergillosis. Pp. 178–181 in M.E. Fowler (ed.), Zoo and Wild Animal Medicine, Current Therapy 3.

Redig, P.T., J.E. Cooper, J.D. Remple and D.B. Hunter (eds.). 1993. Raptor Biomedicine. University of Minnesota Press, Minneapolis.

Remple, J.D. 1993. Raptor bumblefoot: a new treatment technique. Pp. 154–160 in P.T. Redig et al. (eds.), Raptor Biomedicine.

Riddle, K.E. 1981. Surgical treatment of bumblefoot in raptors. Pp. 67–73 in J.E. Cooper and A.G. Greenwood (eds.), Recent Advances in the Study of Raptor Diseases.

Ritchie, B.W., G.J. Harrison and L.R. Harrison (eds.) 1994. Avian Medicine: Principles and Application. Wingers Publishing, Lake Worth, Florida.

Ritchie, B.W., C.M. Otto, K.S. Latimer and D.T. Crowe. 1990. A technique of intraosseous cannulation for intravenous therapy in birds. Compendium of Continuing Education 12: 55–58.

Servheen, C. and W. English. 1979. Movements of rehabilitated bald eagles and proposed seasonal movement patterns of bald eagles in the Pacific Northwest. Raptor Res. 13: 79–88.

Smith, S.A. 1993. Diagnosis and treatment of helminths in birds of prey. Pp. 21–27 in P.T. Redig et al. (eds.), Raptor Biomedicine.

Snelling, J.C. 1975. Raptor rehabilitation at the Oklahoma City Zoo. Raptor Res. 9: 33–45.

Swaim, S.F. and A.H. Lee. 1987. Topical wound medications: A review. J. Am. Vet. Med. Assoc. 190: 1588–1593.

Sweeney, S.J., P.T. Redig and H.B. Tordoff. 1997. Morbidity, survival and productivity of rehabilitated peregrine falcons in the upper midwestern U.S. J. Raptor Res. 31: 347–352.

Tabaka, C.S., J.G. Sikarskie, D.E. Ullrey, S. DeBar and P.K. Ku. 1994. Diet, cast composition, and energy and nutrient intake of red-tailed hawks (Buteo jamaicensis), great horned owls (Bubo virginianus), and turkey vultures (Cathartes aura). Proc. Assoc. Rept. & Amph. Vet. & Amer. Assoc. Zoo Vet.: 290–301.

Wiemeyer, S.N. 1996. Other organochlorine pesticides in birds. Pp. 99–115 in W.N. Beyer et al. (eds.), Environmental Contaminants in Wildlife: Interpreting Tissue Concentrations.

Wimsatt, J., P. Dressen, C. Dennison and S. Turner. 1998. Avian wing bandaging and therapeutic ultrasound treatment. Proc. Amer. Assoc. Zoo Vet. & Amer. Assoc. Wildl. Vet.: 158–159.

Wisecarver, J. and G. Bogue. 1974. Raptor rehabilitation at the Alexander Lindsay Junior Museum. Raptor Res. 8: 6–10.

FURTHER READING AND INTERNET LINKS

Beebe, Frank L. 1992. *The Compleat Falconer.* Hancock House, Blaine, Washington. ISBN 0-88839-253-2.

Beebe, Frank L. 1999. *A Falconry Manual.* Hancock House, Blaine, Washington. ISBN 0-88839-978-2.

Beebe, Frank L. and H.M. Webster. 1994. *North American Falconry and Hunting Hawks.* 7th edition.

Brown, L.H. 1976. *Birds of Prey: Their Biology and Ecology.* Hamlyn. ISBN 0600-313-069.

Brown, L.H. and D. Amadon. 1968. *Eagles, Hawks and Falcons of the World.*

Burnham, Bill. 1997. *A Fascination with Falcons.* Hancock House, Blaine, Washington. ISBN 0-88839-415-2.

Cade, T. 1985. *Falcons of the World.* Cornell University Press. ISBN 0-8014-1454-7.

Cade, T., J.H. Enderson, C.G. Thelander and C.M. White. 1988. *Peregrine Falcon Populations: Their Management and Recovery.* The Peregrine Fund. ISBN 0-9619839-0-6.

Dekker, Dick. 1999. Bolt from the Blue. Hancock House, Blaine, Washington. ISBN 0-88839-434-9.

Fox, N. 1995. *Understanding the Bird of Prey.* Hancock House, Blaine, Washington. ISBN 0- 88839-317-2.

Fox, Nick. 2004. *Classical Falconry: A Treatise on Rook and Crow Hawking.* Hancock House, Blaine, Washington. ISBN 0-88839-548-5.

Haak, Bruce. 1992. *The Hunting Falcon.* Hancock House, Blaine, Washington. ISBN 0-88839-292-3.

Haak, Bruce. 1995. *Pirate of the Plains.* Hancock House, Blaine, Washington. ISBN 0-88839-320-2.

Hollinshead, Martin. 1993. *Hawking Ground Quarry.* Hancock House, Blaine, Washington. ISBN 0-88839-306-7.

Hollinshead, Martin. 1995. *Hawking with Golden Eagles.* Hancock House, Blaine, Washington. ISBN 0-88839-343-1.

Horobin, David. 2004. *Falconry in Literature.* Hancock House, Blaine, Washington. ISBN 0-88839-547-7.

Kotsiopoulos, George. 1999. *Falconry Uncommon.* Hancock House, Blaine, Washington. ISBN 0-88839-450-0.

Maclean, G.L. 1984. *Roberts Birds of Southern Africa.* 5th edition. ISBN 0-620-07681-X.

Martin, S. 1994. The Positive Approach to parrots as pets. Video tapes 1&2. 1. *Understanding Bird Behavior* 2. *Training Through Positive Enforcement.* Natural Encounters. P.O. Box. 68666, Indianapolis, IN 46268.

Parry-Jones. J. 1994. *Training Birds of Prey.* David and Charles, Devon, England. ISBN 0-71530142-X.

Roy III, Joe. 2004. *Duck Hawking and the Art of Falconry.* Hancock House, Blaine, Washington. ISBN 0-88839-553-1.

Upton, Roger. 2002. *Arab Falconry.* Hancock House, Blaine, Washington. ISBN 0-88839-492-6.

van de Wall, J.W.M. 2004. *The Loo Falconry.* Hancock House, Blaine, Washington. ISBN 0-88839-576-0.

Weaver, J.D. and T.J. Cade. *Falcon Propagation: A manual on Captive Breeding.* The Peregrine Fund.

MAGAZINES / PERIODICALS

American Falconry
P.O. Box 187, Dayton, WY 82836-6187
Email: amfalcon@wave.sheridan.wy.us
Homepage: American Falconry Magazine

International Falconer
Turkey Court, Ashford Road, Maidstone, Kent
ME14 5PP England
Email: info@infalconer.com
Homepage: www.intfalconer.com

The Journal of Raptor Research
OSNA, P.O. Box 1897
Lawrence, KS 66044-8897 USA

Journal of Wildlife Rehabilitation
see IWRC (International Wildlife Rehabilitation
Council).

BOOK PUBLISHER

Hancock House Publishers
1431 Harrison Avenue, Blaine, WA 98230-5005
Email: sales@hancockhouse.com
Homepage: www.hancockhouse.com

WEBSITES
[I have listed the websites that I feel are the most comprehensive or the most useful. I have also added links to raptor art websites. The American Falconry website offers many good links—try that first. — R.N.]

www.eagle-hawk.org.au/raptortrack

www.iwrc-online.org

L.L. Electronics (Telemetry Equipment)
Email: LLE@pdnt.com

www.marshallradio.com

www.n-a-f-a.org (North American Falconers
Association)

www.northwoodsfalconry.com

www.nwrawildlife.org
(This site has links to other homepages in the USA,
Canada and Europe.)

www.raptorrecoveryne.org/interlink
(This site has lots of links to rehabilitation centers
worldwide.)

www.vitahawk.com

www.wildfeatherart.com

Aluminium Block Perches
Gary D. Weddle DVM
Home page: http://home.earthlink.net/~eagledoc/

D.B. Scientific
Manufacturers of dietary supplements such as
"Vitahawk" www.vitahawk.com

Falconry Equipment
Homepage: http://members.aol.com/hawkequip/

L.L. Electronics
Makers of outstanding telemetry equipment
Louis Luksander
103 N. Prairieview Road
PO Box 420
Mahomet, Illinois 61853 USA
Email: LLE@pdnt.com

Marshall Radio Telemetry
708 west 1800 North #1
Logan, UT 84321 USA
Phone: (800) 729-7123
Email: info@marshallradio.com
Homepage: Marshall Radio

Northwoods Limited *
(everything you will ever need)
P.O. Box 874
Rainier, WA 98576 USA
Email: northwoods@northwoodsfalconry.com
Homepage: Northwoods Limited

International Wildlife Rehabilitation Council
(IWRC)
Email: iwrc@inreach.com
website: http://www.iwrc-online.org

National Wildlife Rehabilitators Council (NWRA)
Email: nwra@cloudnet.com
Website: http://www.nwrawildlife.org

Independent Bird Register
Email: jenny@ibr.org.uk

INDEX

Italics = table   ***Bold italics*** = illustration or photograph

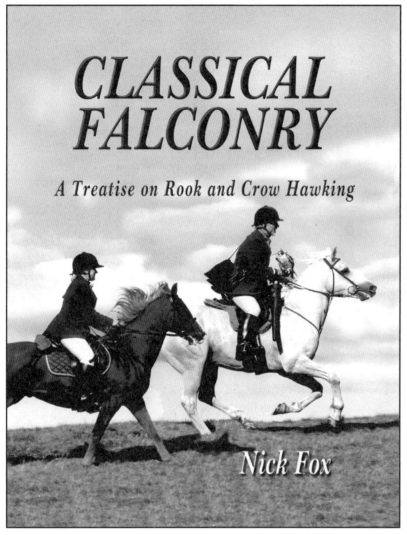

The world leader in birds of prey publishing

Falconry in Literature
David Horobin
ISBN 0-88839-547-7
5½ x 8½, HC, 224 pages

The Loo Falconry:
The Royal Loo Hawking Club
1839-1855
J. W. M. van de Wall
ISBN 0-88839-576-0
8½ x 11, HC, 144 pages

Duck Hawking and
the Art of Falconry
Joe Roy III
ISBN 0-88839-553-1
5½ x 8½, HC, 314 pages

Hawking & Falconry
for Beginners
Adrian Hallgarth
ISBN 0-88839-549-3
5½ x 8½, HC, 208 pages

hancock

house

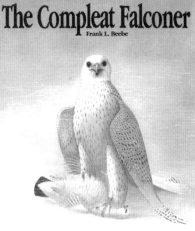

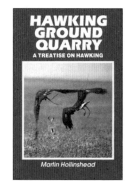
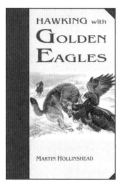